CROSSCURRENTS
PURSUING SOCIAL JUSTICE AND INTERRELIGIOUS WORK
SINCE 1950

CrossCurrents (ISSN 0011-1953; online ISSN 1939-3881) connects the wisdom of the heart with the life of the mind and the experiences of the body. The journal is operated through its parent organization, the Association for Public Religion and Intellectual Life (APRIL), an interreligious network of academics, activists, artists, and community leaders seeking to engage the many ways religion meets the public. Contributions to the journal exist at the nexus of religion, education, the arts, and social justice. The journal is published quarterly on behalf of the Association for Public Religion and Intellectual Life by the University of North Carolina Press.

The Association for Public Religion and Intellectual Life (formerly ARIL) is a global network of leaders, scholars, and social change agents who explore religious life, engage in intellectual inquiry, and lead ethical action in the world today. Their primary objective, especially through annual summer colloquia and *CrossCurrents*, is to bring together leading voices of our time to advocate for justice and to examine global spiritual and interreligious currents in both historical and contemporary perspectives.

A membership to APRIL includes access to *CrossCurrents* starting with Volume 58, 2008, though our partners at Project MUSE, monthly newsletters, early access to summer colloquium themes, a 40% on UNC Press books, and more. For more information, including membership and subscription rates, visit www.aprilonline.org.

This reissue of *CrossCurrents* was one of four issues published in 2020 as part of Volume 70. For a current masthead visit www.aprilonline.org.

© 2020 Association for Public Religion and Intellectual Life. All rights reserved.

ISBN 978-1-4696-6714-0 (Print)

CROSSCURRENTS

PRIVACY

Edited by Yelena Mazour-Matusevich

93
Introduction
Yelena Mazour-Matusevich

95
Privacy, Interiority and Confession: A Historical Perspective
Yelena Mazour-Matusevich

107
Weaponizing Personal Data to Undermine Democracy
Eric Santanen

131
The Surveillance of the Victim: Visibility, Privacy and the Crisis of Bodies in Franciscan Thought
David B. Couturier

145
Whispers in the Closet: Reflections on TSA and Solitude
Taraneh R. Wilkinson

159
Privacy and Digital Life: What Do I Owe My Neighbor
Theresa E. Miedema

200
Notes on Contributors

About the Cover: Copyrights belong to Pierre-Antoine Fabre, EHESS, Paris, France.

CROSSCURRENTS

INTRODUCTION

The central issue of our little volume, which deals with legal and psychological (Taraneh R. Wilkinson), socio-political (Theresa E. Miedema), theological (David B. Couturier), historical (Yelena Mazour-Matusevich), and ethical (Eric Santanen) aspects of privacy and infringements on it, is the uneasy relationship between privacy and security. Both conditions have their own set of risks, which we, as a society and as individuals, must choose, realizing, however, that a risk-free solution to the dilemma privacy versus security does not and cannot exist. Moreover, the arrival of the pandemic has manifold amplified this dilemma, naturally pushing the question of privacy unto the periphery of humanity's concerns, with security taking a quasi-absolute priority. The choice, however difficult, appears to be no longer available or at least temporarily suspended. To surveillance by military intelligence, government administrations, work supervisors, crime investigators, and consumer agencies is now added scrutiny due to the outbreak of coronavirus. On one hand, the Fourth Amendment, which states that "the right of the people to be secure in their persons, houses, papers, and effects, against reasonable searches and seizures, shall not be violated," hardly means anything during an epidemic. Yet, on the other hand, what does the "the right to be let alone" stand for in the situation when one is forced to stay alone and isolated? Our preferences, choices, beliefs, and inhibitions do not matter. "We" takes over "I" when we must put aside our differences and mobilize against an invisible, indifferent, and invincible (as far as the possibility to destroy it goes) enemy, which, for the sake of evolution, can strike all and kills the weakest. When survival is in question, personal sensibilities and comforts must take the backstage, while prohibitions, mass lockdowns, curfews, border closures, triage, mandatory temperature taking, quarantines, and hospitalizations must be accepted with cooperation. We all understand this. Even the most obdurate gun enthusiast understands that he cannot shoot the virus. When scared and sick, we all submit to

INTRODUCTION

whatever government measures there are if they promise to save us. For now, for a while, until things go back to normal. But will they? Will we get back whatever small amount of privacy was left before the outbreak? Will we care to get it back? Will we cherish it more? The pandemic will leave behind scarred citizens and battered state structures, the first realizing their utter vulnerability and the second both their inadequacy and great power. Although the human ability to learn nothing from the past and forget useful experiences soon after they pass should not be underestimated, some habits learned during the crisis might not go away. The crisis has already forced us "beyond abstract discussions of privacy rights" toward "the need for a new and more vibrant social ethic," as David B. Couturier put it in his article here. If anything, our reliance on technology, as well as our exposure to it, has greatly increased during our quarantines and lockdowns. In this new context, words from the title of Taraneh R. Wilkinson's piece, "whispers," "closet," "reflections," and "solitude," now sound like a description of our daily lives. Those from Theresa E. Miedema's essay "What Do I Owe My Neighbor" and Eric Santanen's article "Weaponizing Personal Data to Undermine Democracy" sound not only like calls for action but rally cries for a just war to preserve at least something holy in our distorted reality, which, for the sake of safety might end up losing all beauty and dignity that make life human. In any case, the struggle between the need for privacy and the need for security, exacerbated by the current crisis, is likely to remain intense, keeping the concerns and perspectives gathered in this volume not less but more relevant for a good while to come.

—*Yelena Mazour-Matusevich*

CROSSCURRENTS

PRIVACY, INTERIORITY AND CONFESSION
A Historical Perspective

Yelena Mazour-Matusevich

Introduction

This historical inquiry focuses on the connection between the increasing interiority of a religious experience, confession, and the development of privacy, and aims to demonstrate how certain innovations in pastoral care and new approaches to contemplative practices led to the emergence of privacy as a condition of confession and penance, and, therefore, of salvation itself. Using Michel Foucault's theoretical framework, as well as primary historical sources from the late fourteenth, fifteenth, and sixteenth centuries, this essay argues that developments in introspection and a more personalized approach to confessional practices in late medieval-early modern times resulted in a tension between privacy and safety, which is highly relevant today.

The major difficulty in exploring the connection between interiority and privacy results from a lack of a clear definition of either concept. There is no generally accepted definition of interiority, which is sometimes called interiorization, subjectivization, individualization, individuation,[1] or "un certain movement intériorisant dans le christianisme," according to the expression of Jacques Derrida.[2] The same goes for privacy, which can be understood in judicial, psychological, economic, political, ethical, and other terms. However, as important as it is to formulate these concepts' meanings, the lack of mathematical precision in their definitions should not hinder the discussion undertaken in this volume, for, as Aristotle rightly put it, in human affairs "we must be satisfied with the broad outline of the truth [...]"[3.]

For our purposes, the examination of privacy from the judicial point of view, as presented by Dr. Theresa E. Miedema in her article in this volume,[4.] offers a sufficient starting point, since some contemporary definitions and insights into this issue turn out to be surprisingly relevant for contextualizing late medieval-early modern pastoral concerns for the modern reader. Thus, Dean Prosser's analysis of the case law related to privacy,[5.] which "was adopted by the *Restatement (Second) of Torts* (2010), and has been widely endorsed in Canadian and American jurisprudence,"[6.] is fairly applicable to the late medieval-early modern concerns with privacy examined in this essay. Among the four torts related to the privacy case and examined by Prosser, two—public disclosure of embarrassing private facts and publicity that puts the plaintiff in a false light in the public eye—are not only relatable to the historical period in question, but also, as we shall see, correspond to apprehensions concerning privacy of confession as articulated by clergy at the time. By the same token, in a leading UK case related to the tort of breach of confidence *Campbell v. MGN Ltd*, Lord Nicholls' observation that "[a] proper degree of privacy is essential for the [well-being] and development of an individual"[7.] is remarkably consistent with both the early modern assessment of the issue and historical anthropology's view of privacy as a precondition to personhood.

The turn inward
The spirituality of the late medieval-early modern period is commonly associated with the "turn inward," which gradually became synonymous with the beginning of self-formation in what Foucault identified as the "genealogy of the modern subject."[8.] Both the Protestant and Catholic faiths came to place a greater emphasis on interiority, testifying to a "massive subjective turn of modern culture, a new form of inwardness, in which we come to think of ourselves as beings with inner depths."[9.] While this process remains "all but clear-cut and easily comprehensible,"[10.] scholars have recognized several criteria, or triggers formative for future developments, of introspection in late medieval Christianity. Among them are innovations in pastoral care, creative approaches to contemplative practices, the transfer of monastic methods to laity, and the

reworking of earlier historical models of auto-exteriorization.[11.] Auto-exteriorization is understood as the process of consciously and voluntarily (not under duress) expressing, in oral or written form, in public or in private, thoughts and feelings, which were up until this point known only to their beholder. Michel Foucault identified three historical models of auto-exteriorization in the Western world: the classical Greco-Roman "gnomic self," from the Greek *gnomé*, meaning coincidence of will and knowledge;[12.] the dramatic public exteriorization of sins called *exomologesis*; and the Christian monastic technic of *exagoreusis*, consisting in an intentional verbalization of one's thoughts to a trusted spiritual adviser. As an example of the first case, Foucault analyzes Seneca's practice of daily self-questioning found in *De ira*. This practice is not a means of discovering some hidden mystical truth about oneself, but rather serves to compare two accounts: one is what the person had done during the day and the other what he should have done. The discrepancy between the two is the subject of self-examination with the goal of improving one's behavior in the future. Jörg Rüpke identified this model as a "representative individuality,"[13.] whose aim is "not individual difference but perfection in fulfilling a social or religious role."[14.] Even when this procedure is exteriorized through sharing one's questions with another person, as in the example of Seneca's young friend Serenus, it changes nothing in its nature, since it remains entirely within the framework of correspondence between knowledge and will. Such a self-examination is not to be confused with Christian introspection, as in cases of St. Augustine's *Confessions* or as described, for example, in the fifteenth-century manual by an abbot Garcia Jimenes de Cisneros (1455-1510): "[...] see briefly how thou hast spent the day, and ask forgiveness of God making ty confession."[15.]

The second model is *exomologesis*,[16.] which encompasses "everything that the penitent does to obtain his reconciliation during the time when he retains the status of penitent,"[17.] amounting to a highly theatrical act of showing oneself to a community of believers in order to secure pardon. To be sure, privacy has not always been a prerequisite of Christian confession and penance, which used to be one and the same thing. The scriptural premise "If we confess our sins, he is faithful and just, and will forgive our sins and cleanse us from all unrighteousness" (1 John 1:9) does not, by itself, require or presuppose privacy of confession. Quite to the contrary, public acknowledgement of guilt and its public expiation through the demonstration of penance were generally required for the absolution of sins as a condition for the readmission of a sinner into the Christian community:

> Christianity from the first applied austere standards of behavior, and in the course of its advance in the Graeco-Roman world developed a discipline for the correction of Christians who violated the code. In the first stage this took the form of public confession, made before the assembled congregation. In graver offenses and in cases of impenitence or of public scandal, this discipline was accompanied by a period of exclusion from the fellowship [...] The word *exomologesis* is used to include both confession and penance which are parts of the same process of public humiliation.[18.]

The third model of *exagoreusis*, which Foucault describes based on John Cassian's *Institutiones* and *Collationes*, consists in testing "the nature, the quality, the substance of his [monk's] thoughts," rather than actions,[19.] by "telling them to a master or a spiritual father."[20.] This model is of relevance here, as it is closely related to confessions, examinations of conscience, and directions of souls, which have been singled out as important interiorization technics because they "subjected a practitioner to pastoral authority at the same time that they created these subjects as unique individuals."[21.] Late medieval and early modern confessional manuals are collections of such technics designed to regulate confessant's and confessor's behaviors, and to address difficulties in evaluating actions revealed at confessions, for example, the problem of scrupulous conscience that rigorous examinations of conscience tended to produce.

The term *scrupuli* was used in the Middle Ages to describe exaggeratedly anxious agitations of the soul caused by the idea of a moral or religious insufficiency of its bearer. The increased emphasis on introspection led to a growing concern for moral scruples, which is registered in late medieval-early modern theological literature. Leading theological authorities of the time, such as the chancellor of the University of Paris, Jean Gerson (1363-1429), the leader of the Dominican Observant movement, Saint Antoninus of Florence (1389-1459), the famous Strasbourg preacher, Johannes Geiler von Kaysererg (1445-1510), the Dominican theologian Sylvestro Mazzolini or Pririas (1456/1457-1527), Thomas More, Martin Luther (in whom scrupulosity famously attains the degree of acute anxiety), and the official father of Christian probabilism, Bartolomè de Medina (1527-1580), to name just few, dedicated considerable attention to this problem. Thus, Johannes Geiler von Kayserberg, whose concern with confession went hand in hand with his desire to develop "l'homme interieur"[22.] in his listeners, believed confession to be an act of both penance and consolation, with purification and comfort leading to an overall improvement of the penitent's spiritual well-being. Sylvestro Mazzolini, an austere Dominican "scarcely ever in doubt,"[23.] also emphasized the danger of too scrupulous a conscience, promoting the gentleness of a confessor in his role as a bringer of comfort to the faithful in his 1514 manual *Summa Sylvestrina*. He states that excessive questioning of the confessant should be omitted, "lest the confessor molests the penitent unnecessarily."[24.] Among the qualities required of a good confessor are tactfulness, gentleness, and trustworthiness so that "[...] the penitents do not fear that if they tell their sins, the confessor afterward will be hateful or contemptuous or accusatory toward them. Rather, he should love them the more tenderly as cherished offspring who have committed themselves totally to his trust."[25.] Defender of American Indians, Bartolomeo de Las Casas (1474 or 1484-1566), promoted an idea similar to consolatory confession in his own manual *Avisos y reglas para confesores de españoles* (*Admonitions and Regulations for the Confessors of Spaniards*), to be used by priests in his diocese in New Spain.[26.] Concerned with the problem of moral scrupulosity, Spanish theologian Bartolomè de Medina introduced, in his *Breve istruttione de confessor*, a special type of "patient," whom he called "scrupolosi & pusillanimi," "scrupulous and timorous," whose ills, "among other infirmities [...] are very difficult to cure, need great remedies, and a physician of great science and experience [...]"[27.]

Changes in confessional practices

Such a physician was to be the confessor, who should be specifically trained to address the psychological needs and difficulties of the growing number of laity embracing the contemplative life. While confession was not required of all Christians until the thirteenth century, and even then was typically practiced just once per year, founder of the Company of Jesus, Ignatius of Loyola (1491-1556), incorporated consolatory and frequent (monthly) confession into his *Spiritual Exercises*, through which it became a fundamental part of Jesuit teachings. Already *Formula of the*

Institute, which Ignatius composed in 1539, presented to Pope Paul III, and reworked, together with his companions, for the approval of Pope Julius II in 1550, specified as one of the purposes of the new Jesuit order "the spiritual consolation of Christ's faithful through hearing confessions."[28.] Early Jesuits, such as Jeronimo Nadal (1507-1580), saw themselves primarily as spiritual physicians and consolers, while Nicolas Bobadilla (1511-1590), who was one of the first to join Loyola in 1533, went even further than the founder by advocating daily confession and communion. It was also the Jesuits who transformed confession from a rare and almost unknown spiritual ritual into "one practiced by students, noblemen, women and Jesuit seminarians."[29.] The unprecedented expansion of confession and the emphasis on its fundamental importance in Christian life elevated the status of confessor and set out to forge more intimate relationships between members of the laity and the clergy.

Although early modern Christianity "inherited a benevolent medieval tradition that described the confessor as a physician, and the sacrament as a font of encouragement, consolation and healing,"[30.] the new emphasis on privacy in the direction of conscience stands in sharp contrast to the public self-revelations of earlier *exomologesis* practices, which put "under everybody's eyes the flesh, the body, which has committed the sin [...] showing the sinner"[31.] to the community. Indeed, if *exomologesis* meant that in order to be reintegrated the sinner had to become highly visible in his community in the most direct and physical manner, late medieval-early modern manuals for confessors clearly attest that communal reintegration required the highest possible degree of private introspection and social invisibility of the penitent. Thus, the main requirement of a confessor, according to the late medieval theologian Jean Gerson, is an extreme discretion without which "it would be better for the confessor to die than to reveal anything said to him."[32.] While public self-humiliation used to be the communal act of humility par excellence, in the late medieval period public humility began to be seen as no humility at all. In fact, the very fact of publicity appears to disqualify penitence as unauthentic or worse. Only restrain, discretion, and moderation are signs of true humility, while deficiency in these attributes signals falsehood or even diabolic pride: "The second sign for genuine spiritual currency is the discretion [...] which is the daughter of humility. Of people [who lack discretion] I say that they will quickly fall for every demoniacal illusion."[33.] One can only imagine how such a perception, championed by the intellectual elite of professional theologians, clashed with ancient popular practices, while also bringing all kinds of categories of people and phenomena under suspicion.

The concern for privacy also surfaces in relation to the system of penance, which had existed for centuries and involved a period of public penitence and exclusion from communion with or without simultaneous banishment from a local community. These traditional measures also belong to the process of *exomologesis*, which had strong communal support and was, therefore, harder to address and eliminate. Nevertheless, these customs too began to provoke theological criticism. Thus, the preoccupation to avoid public shaming of the penitent, and aversion to publicity in general, is a consistent theme in highly influential advisory manuals by the chancellor of the University of Paris Jean Gerson, who categorically opposed public penance even for the most severe crimes, such as infanticide, as an "enormitatem et inhumanem ac bestialem crudelitatem," an "enormous, inhumane and bestial cruelty," claiming that one should refrain from adding further affliction to those who are already afflicted enough, "ut quid, igitur afflicto superaddatur afflictio."[34.]

There is, however, another rationale that lies beneath the campaign for increased confidentiality and secrecy in confessional and penitential practices. Privacy of confessions and penances was to be preserved as much in order to avoid creating a public scandal as to avoid harming the penitent. Thus, formulating his stunningly lenient policy, considering modern debates on this topic, on the question of infanticide and abortion in his treatise *De potestate absolvendi*, Gerson states that "The case of abortions, whether in the belly or outside of it, which occur completely unintentionally from the part of the parent, should be dismissed by bishops, and maximally so if they are secret in order not to scandalize other people."[35.] Centuries old *exomologesis*-related practices are thus transformed from widely accepted healing rituals into scandals, deprived of spiritual benefits for both individuals and communities alike. A century after Gerson, one finds the same horror of public scandal in a moderate Lutheran theologian, Philip Melanchthon: "he who violates human tradition does not sin so long as a scandal does not arise from it."[36.] Eventually, although not in a straightforward fashion, the obsession with privacy in matters of confession and penitence led, both in Catholic and Protestant churches, to policies aiming for a complete and final dismissal of all expressions of *exomologesis*.

The tendency of late medieval-early modern pastoral theology to discourage opportunities of public exposure and scandal resulted in criticism of the common practice of reserving the absolution of some grave sins for higher church authorities, such as bishops. Leading theologians of the time rejected this practice precisely on the grounds that a modern jurist, in the earlier mentioned citation, would qualify as two main infringements (torts) on privacy: "public disclosure of embarrassing private facts" and putting "the plaintiff in a false light in the public eye." Reserving sins for higher authorities to absolve risked exposing penitents to their communities, due to the high probability that a penitent's journey to such an authority or a visit from there of would be public knowledge, and thus constituted an obvious breach of the secret of confession. Even an eventuality of such a breach made this practice unacceptable to new sensibilities of the late medieval-early modern clergy, as is evident from Jean Gerson's 1406 letter to a bishop: "We must take into account also the sense of modesty and concern for reputation in women or their relatives, if women frequently either publically or from a great distance are sent to confessors. [...] What good does it do—certainly it does great harm—to add one source of shame to another, one more heavy burden upon the burden and difficulty of confessing such sins?"[37.] The already mentioned Sylvestro Mazzolini shared this sentiment and argued for the complete abolition of this custom. Likewise, Dutch theologian Godescale or Godescalc Rosemondt (d. 1526) protested an unreasonably great number of confession cases reserved for bishops,[38.] deploring, in his *Confessionale*, the negative effects that such practices tend to have on penitents. Yet, the opposition to publicity was not universal and encountered resistance. For example, Carlo Borromeo (1538-1584) extensively used the tradition of reserving the absolution of grave sins for the higher office of bishops, that is for his own. It is telling, however, that his practice provoked the indignation of many among the Milanese clergy, city government, and population, who found the reserved cases too many and penances too severe and disproportioned to the sins committed. Among those who opposed Borromeo's policies was the Jesuit preacher Julio Mazzarino, who claimed that this policy created needless desperation among penitents, confusion among confessors, and scandal in the city of Milan.[39.]

Once again, both personal distress (desperation and confusion) on the individual level and social distress (scandal) on the collective level are perceived as the grounds for the discontinuation of this traditional practice.

Conclusion

Privacy is not a universal concept. It is neither natural nor ahistorical. Increased introspection, confidentiality, and privacy only gradually gained ground in Christian religious life, with a marked change in attitudes in late medieval-early modern times. New approaches to confession and penance both signal and shape this change. We might choose to look at this process as progress, but whether it had a positive or negative impact on large-scale societal dynamics in late medieval-early modern Europe and on Christianity-influenced cultures in general is another question. Surely, we shudder at the thought of public confession and penance, while the notion that verbalization of a self-reflection (*veridiction*, in Foucault's terms) carries a self-forming potential is dear to our modern minds. Discreet, individual, and private religious experiences described in late medieval-early modern confessional manuals and theological treatises validate the modern view of privacy as a precondition to personhood, which we consider a good thing. However, we must acknowledge that the manuals and treatises analyzed in this essay were written by members of the social intellectual elite, while the late medieval-early modern shift toward interiority and privacy in spiritual matters produced multifaceted and even controversial consequences for the general population. *Exomologesis*, which functioned as a channel of reabsorption of penitents back into the collective, did not have "as its function the establishment of personal identity."[40.] In fact, it served as one of the mechanisms of reinforcing communal identity as a whole. The rejection of this and similar communal practices resulted in the increasing exclusion of the community from the spiritual process, promoting a special and intimate relationship between individual community members and trained professional confessors. The elimination, or official distrust, of ancient practices on the part of theologians, both Catholic inquisitors and Protestant clergy, clashed with popular sensibilities and provoked resentment at the growing lack of moral and spiritual control on the part of community members. The exclusion of the community also greatly increased clerical control over individuals, which led to abuses of confessants. While some clergy emphasized compassion and forgiveness, and faithfully kept secret what they heard at confessions, others exploited their power and used the information captured during the sacrament for personal gain or to inform civil authorities, as it happened, to give a more recent example, in many despotic regimes of the twentieth century. Young children, who were not subjected to confession during the medieval period until the age of ten or twelve, as they were deemed incapable of sinning in any meaningful way before this age, were gradually forced to confess much earlier, often even before their confirmation. This practice led to increased intimacy with priests and sexual abuse of minors, which often begins within the penitent-confessor relationship. While we deplore these unfortunate developments, we are forced to admit that they result, deep down, from a potentially unresolvable dilemma of the negative correlation between privacy and safety. Regardless of how we choose to evaluate the pastoral efforts of our intellectual ancestors, it is evident that about six hundred years ago they began to regard privacy of internal life as vital for a person's psychological and spiritual well-being, and as such worthy of protection from various forms of public embarrassment and exposure. The late medieval-early modern campaign for a more frequent, more internalized, and more thorough form of confession for the laity led to a further interiorization of faith, an increased self-awareness accompanied by painful moral *scrupuli*, and a growing concern, on the part of the theologians, for the confidentiality of this sacrament and the privacy of ensuing penitence. These develpments had an important, and possibly even a formative, bearing on the emergence of the concept of privacy, which is deeply rooted in the theological foundation of our civilization.

Notes

1. Otto, Bernd-Christian, 2017, "Magic and Religious Individualization: On the Construction and Deconstruction of Analytical Categories in the Study of Religion," *Historia Religionum*, 9, pp. 29-52.
2. Derrida, Jacques, Vattimo, Gianni, *La Religion* (Paris: Seuil, 1996), p. 20.
3. Aristotle, *Nicomachean Ethics* (Penguin), reprint 1975, p. 65.
4. See Miedema, Theresa E, "Privacy and Digital Life: What Do I Owe My Neighbor," in this volume.
5. Prosser, William, *Privacy*, (1960) 48 Cal. L. Rev. 383.
6. Miedema, T. E., "Privacy and Digital Life."
7. *Campbell v MGN Ltd*, [2004] UKHL 22, [2004] 2 AC 457 at para 12 per Lord Nicholls, quoted by T. E. Miedema, "Privacy and Digital Life."

8. Foucault, Michel, *About the Beginning of the Hermeneutics of the Self: Lectures at Dartmouth College*, 1980, trans. Graham Burchell, ed. Henri-Paul Fruchard and Daniele Lorenzini (Chicago: Chicago University Press, 2016), p. 201.
9. Taylor, Charles, *The Ethics of Authenticity* (Cambridge, Massachusetts and London: Harvard University Press, 1991), p. 26.
10. Otto, B-C., "Magic and Religious Individualization," p. 33.
11. See Sluhovsky, Moshe, "The Birth of a Modern Introspective Self" and Rob Faesen's "The Turn to Interiority in the Early Modern Period," trans. John Arblaster, in *The Crisis of Religion and the Problem of Roman Catholic Self-Definition* (New York/Leiden: Brill, forthcoming).
12. Foucault, *About the Beginning of the Hermeneutics of the Self: Lectures at Dartmouth College*, p. 209-10.
13. Jörg, Rüpke, Introduction to *The Individual in the Religions of the Ancient Mediterranean* (Oxford: Oxford University Press, 2013).
14. Foucault, *About the Beginning of the Hermeneutics*, p. 206.
15. Cisneros, Garcia Jimenes de, *Book of Exercises for the Spiritual Life*, London, 1876, Chapter 21, p. 84.
16. Foucault, *About the Beginning of the Hermeneutics*, p. 212-14.
17. Foucault, *About the Beginning of the Hermeneutics*, p. 214.
18. McNeill, John, and Gamer, Helena, *Medieval Hand-Books of Penance* (New York: Octagon, 1965), p. 4, 8 and 14.
19. Foucault, *About the Beginning of the Hermeneutics*, p. 216-17.
20. Foucault, *About the Beginning of the Hermeneutics*, p. 219.
21. Sluhovsky, Moshe, "The Birth of a Modern Introspective Self," Brown University Concentration in Contemplative Studies and Department of Religious Studies public lecture, Friday, September 16, 2016.
22. Arnaud, Matthieu, *Annoncer l'Evangile (xve-xviie siècles). Permanences et mutations de la prédication*, Paris, Le Cerf, 2006, p. 251.
23. McDonnell, Kilian, 1993, "The Summae Confessorum on the Integrity of Confession as Prolegomena for Luther and Trent," *Theological Studies*, 54, pp. 405-25, p. 422.
24. Mazzolini, Sylvester, *Summa summarum in Summa sylvestrina*, 2 vols., 1593, cited by K. McDonnell, "The Summae Confessorum...", p. 422.
25. Gerson, Jean, *On the Art of Hearing Confessions*, Brian Patrick McGuire, *Jean Gerson: Early Works* (New York: Paulist Press Early Works, 1998), p. 368. The theme is found in Gerson's vernacular works, such as *Note sur la confession, Œuvres completes de Jean Gerson*, ed. Palémon Glorieux (Paris [etc.]: Desclée, 1960-1973, volume 7: part one: p. 412): "Que les curés et gens d'Eglise qui a ce sont ordonnez, mettent diligence a traiter doulcement tous ceux qui se confessent..." Further on referred to as OC: volume number: page number.
26. Tentler, Thomas, *Sin and Confession on the Eve of the Reformation* (Princeton, NJ: Princeton University Press, 1977), p. 367.
27. Medina, Bartolomè de, *Breve istruttione de' confessori, come si debba amministrare il Sacramento della Penitentia* (Salamanca: 1579, Roma: 1588), p. 220 and p. 222: "fra le altre infermità [...] che nell'anima sono di cura difficilissima, et hanno bisogno di rimedij grandi, et di medico di grande scienza & esperienza [...]"

28. Maher, Michael, "Confession and consolation: the Society of Jesus and its promotion of the general confession," in Parker, Kenneth L. and Thayer, Anne T. (eds.) *Penitence in the Age of Reformations* (Aldershot: Ashgate, 2000), pp. 184-200, p. 184. John O'Malley, *The First Jesuits* (Cambridge, MA: Harvard University Press. 1993), pp. 82-83: "Consolation—few terms appear more often in early Jesuit documents. Sometimes it is simply a conventional greeting and means not much more than "blessings."
29. O'Malley, *The First Jesuits*, p.186.
30. Fleming, Julia, *Defending Probabilism: The Moral Theology of Juan Caramuel* (Washington, DC: Georgetown University Press, 2006), p. 3.
31. Foucault, *About the Beginning of the Hermeneutics*, p. 214.
32. Gerson, *On the Art of Hearing Confessions*, McGuire, *Early Works*, p. 368.
33. Gerson, *On Distinguishing Revelations*, McGuire, *Early Works*, p. 343.
34. Claude Gauvard and Gilbert Ouy, "Gerson et l'infanticide, défense des femmes et critique de la pénitence publique," in *"Riens ne m'est seur que la chose incertaine" : études sur l'art d'écrire au Moyen Age offertes à Eric Hicks par ses élèves, collègues, amies et amis*, publiées par Jean-Claude Mühlethaler et Denis Billotte, (Geneva: Slatkine, 2001), pp. 45-66, p. 51.
35. Jean Gerson, *Œuvres complètes*, Palémon Glorieux (ed.), Paris [etc.], Desclée, 1960-1973, OC: 9, p. 422: "Casus abortuum, vel in ventre vel extra, qui veniunt omnino praeter intentionem parentem, dimittendi sunt curatis, maxime si sunt secreti, nec proximos scandalizant [...]"
36. Philipp Melanchthon, *Common Places: Loci Communes 1521*, ed. Christian Preus (St. Louis: Concordia Publishing, 2014), p. 86.
37. Gerson, Letter 24 to a bishop, 1408, McGuire, *Early Works*, p. 241 & p. 243. Gerson addresses this issue in *De potestate absolvendi et paccatorum reservatione*, OC 9: 421. On the issue of reserved sins see Wietse de Boer, "The Politics of the Soul: Confession in Counter-Reformation Milan", in: *Penitence in the Age of Reformations*, in Kenneth L. Parker and Anne T. Thayer (eds.) (Aldershot: Ashgate, 2000), pp. 116-33.
38. Dorothy Catherine Brown, *Pastor and Laity in the Theology of Jean Gerson* (Cambridge: Cambridge University Press, 1987), p. 72.
39. See Flavio Rurale, "Carlo Borromeo, Botero, Mazzarino: incontri e scontri nella ridefinizione del potere sacerdotale e della politica "moderna", in Carlo Borromeo e l'opera della "Grande Riforma." *Cultura, religione e arti del governo nella Milano del pieno Cinquecento*, ed. F. Buzzi and D. Zardin (Milano: Credito Artigiano, 1997), pp. 289-302.
40. Foucault, *About the Beginning of the Hermeneutics*, p. 215.

CROSSCURRENTS

WEAPONIZING PERSONAL DATA TO UNDERMINE DEMOCRACY

Eric Santanen

Not only does life tend to keep us actively busy, but the intensity of that activity seems to escalate over time as families grow and careers progress. In response, we tend to gravitate toward products and services that emphasize "convenience" and efficiency in our lives. More and more, we turn to digital technologies in order to manage the complexity of our daily routines, schedule our activities, purchase products, and keep in touch with one another. The driving force behind our willingness to adopt various technologies appears to be our collective and relentless search for convenience. These conveniences allow us to communicate with people more efficiently, to search for information with greater ease, and to complete certain tasks more quickly than ever before. As our schedules intensify, we seek these conveniences at any price. At the same time, however, we often fail to acknowledge the true cost for all of our presumed technological conveniences: our personal privacy. Perhaps this failure occurs because, unlike money, people don't have "privacy wallets." Privacy, in this context, has no physical manifestation that can be counted and inventoried. As a result, it appears to be the perfect transactional medium – it seems never to run out like the money in our wallet does. Similarly, we don't receive periodic statements from our "privacy bank" indicating the amount of privacy that we have left, or alerting us that we've overdrawn our privacy account.

Since we so readily barter with our privacy, it seems useful to have a better understanding of what privacy is and why we should value it.

Other questions occur, such as: What problems occur when we "spend" our privacy? And why should we protect this free-to-acquire and seemingly limitless resource? Understanding the phenomenon of privacy and addressing these questions requires an exploration that begins with an appreciation for the philosophical foundations of privacy. Next, this paper explores various ways in which our privacy is compromised and how ensuing activities can be used to manipulate our thoughts and actions, often without our specific awareness. Finally, this paper presents a set of recommendations that are useful to help preserve privacy and protect personal data so that we are less open to abuse and manipulation.

Privacy and human dignity
Warren and Brandeis (1890) were among the first to make a coherent argument for the legal protection of personal privacy. This argument revolved around what they described as the "inviolate personality" and was an articulation of the right of the individual to enjoy a life that is free from the unwanted intrusion of others. In order to enjoy life, they reasoned, it is necessary for people to have "the right to be let alone" and cast this right as a protection for personal liberty. Capturing sentiments that are as relevant today as they were over a century ago, Warren and Brandeis noted:

> The intensity and complexity of life, attendant upon advancing civilization, have rendered necessary some retreat from the world, and man, under the refining influence of culture, has become more sensitive to publicity, so that solitude and privacy have become more essential to the individual; but modern enterprise and invention have, through invasions upon his privacy, subjected him to mental pain and distress, far greater than could be inflicted by mere bodily injury. (p. 196)

Warren and Brandeis framed the right to privacy as a right against the world, specifically as the "right of the individual to be let alone." Violations of this right, they argued, result in a lowering of social standards and of morality in ways that belittle the individual by inverting the relative importance of things, thus dwarfing the thoughts and aspirations of a people.

Philosopher Edward Bloustein extended Warren & Brandeis' seminal work with the assertion that privacy is the definitive construct behind human individuality, freedom, and liberty. Reflecting on various cultural and historical events, Bloustein argued (1964):

> The fundamental fact is that our Western culture defines individuality as including the right to be free from certain types of intrusions. This measure of personal isolation and personal control over the conditions of its abandonment is of the very essence of personal freedom and dignity, is part of what our culture means by these concepts. A man whose home may be entered at the will of another, whose conversation may be overheard at the will of another, whose marital and familial intimacies may be overseen at the will of another is less of a man, has less human dignity, on that account. He who may intrude upon another at will is the master of the other and, in fact, intrusion is a primary weapon of the tyrant. (p. 165)

Bloustein argues that privacy and its influence on personal dignity is valuable to society because it helps people understand themselves as social beings in the context of various types of relationships that they enjoy. These relationships are fundamentally altered when private life is held up to public scrutiny. As anonymity that was once enjoyed is replaced by notoriety, confidences can become violated, and ultimately, people are less masters of their own destinies without privacy. Accordingly, privacy violations undermine human dignity by restricting personal freedoms and demeaning individuality. He further notes that injury to the person as a result of violating privacy occurs *even when the person is unaware* of such intrusion. A final and lasting consequence of intruding on privacy is that once harmed, an individual's dignity cannot be repaired.

Nearly seventy years after Warren and Brandies published their paper, Bloustein had greater exposure to new technologies and was able to see more clearly the specific impacts that computerized data gathering activities have on individuals: "... the fear that a private life may be turned into a public spectacle is greatly enhanced when the lurid facts have been reduced to key punches or blips on a magnetic tape accessible ... to any clerk..." (p. 191).

Philosopher Richard Wasserstrom (1978) also had concerns about data storage technologies and how they might impact our privacy. He pointed out that simply storing confidential information in a data bank necessarily makes that information less confidential because it is now possible for that information to be disclosed to persons other than those to whom disclosure was intended (p. 326). While this immediately conjures thoughts of identity theft or hacking one's bank account, the potential abuses of this data extend far beyond these immediate abuses. Wasserstrom continues this theme by noting "…ones fears, fantasies, jealousies, and desires—are often embarrassing if disclosed to others than those to whom we choose to disclose them" (p. 330). In this context, it is trivial to see how the desire to protect our fears, fantasies, desires, or just about any other type of personal information is a powerful motivator for our actions. In short, access to personal information makes us vulnerable to various kinds of manipulation.

Privacy and overt manipulation

Long before computers were used to gather information about personal behavior, insights gained through more traditional surveillance activities were used to coerce individuals to act in certain ways. While this type of activity is hardly new in society, it can have startling impact with implications that extend far beyond the targeted individual. It is well documented that the FBI, suspecting his ties to communism, surveilled Dr. Martin Luther King Jr. (Gage 2014). While no evidence related to communism emerged, the FBI did discover evidence of his extra-marital affair which was subsequently used to manipulate his actions with the intention to undermine the Civil Rights Movement. A letter addressed to Dr. King, written by the FBI, was constructed so that it appeared to come from a follower of the Movement and threated to reveal Dr. King's extra-marital activities:

> No person can overcome the facts, not even a fraud like yourself. Lend your sexually psychotic ear to the enclosure. You will find yourself and in all your dirt, filth, evil and moronic talk exposed on the record for all time…. Listen to yourself, you filthy, abnormal animal. You are on the record.

The conclusion of this letter then escalated to the point of suggesting Dr. King should commit suicide prior to the Civil Rights March on Washington D.C. in August of 1963.

> King, there is only one thing left for you to do. You know what it is. You have just 34 days in which to do it (this exact number has been selected for a specific reason, it has definite practical significance). You are done. There is but one way out for you. You better take it before your filthy, abnormal fraudulent self is bared to the nation.

Privacy and covert manipulation

The example above dramatically portrays how damaging information from our past can be used to manipulation our future actions. Clearly, behavior that violates social norms or deviates from specific virtues can be used against us. Indeed, many will use the example above as the intrinsic motivation for leading an exemplary life at all times. This logic is difficult to refute. However, information about us does not have to be particularly salacious or even embarrassing in order for us to be open to manipulation. Harm to an individual's dignity can be particularly effective even if the targeted individual remains unaware of the specific of the manipulation as Bloustein highlighted.

Using even the most mundane personal data to manipulate individual behavior are relatively simple in a world where personal data are merely the byproduct of living in an information age. Whether this data is used by the organization that originally gathered it or by third party hackers makes no practical difference: the mere existence of large volumes of data about each of us creates personal vulnerabilities that are impossible to defend against.

In January 2012, Facebook data scientist Adam Kramer ran an experiment that manipulated the news feeds of nearly 700,000 Facebook users. The specific intention of the research was to determine the extent to which emotional states of users can be transferred to others, leading people to experience the same emotions without their specific awareness. Essentially, the researchers wanted to know how easily people could be manipulated without their knowledge of being manipulated. The results were both illuminating and alarming: "When positive expressions were reduced, people produced fewer positive posts and more negative posts; when negative expressions were reduced, the opposite pattern occurred. These results indicate that emotions expressed by others on Facebook influence our own emotions, constituting experimental evidence for massive-scale contagion via social networks" (Kramer *et al.* 2014). Boiling it all down, Facebook demonstrated just how easily and effectively it could manipulate the mood and subsequent behavior of unsuspecting users simply by altering the theme of the messages (positive or negative in tone) they were exposed to while using the Facebook system.

The publication of this study by the Proceedings of the National Academy of Sciences also caused its editors to publish a rare and formal "Editorial Expression of Concern" regarding the study and the extent to which Facebook users were aware of the manipulation (Verma 2014). The authors noted in their paper, "[The work] was consistent with Facebook's Data Use Policy, to which all users agree prior to creating an account on Facebook, constituting informed consent for this research." It seems, however, that there is some disparity concerning this portion of Facebook's user policy. The active user policy at the time the study was conducted did not include any language about user information being used for research purposes. It was not until May of 2012, several months *after* the study had concluded, that Facebook updated its user policy to introduce details about conducting research with user data (Hill 2014). Ignoring the details concerning which user policy was active at the time, this study raised a number of concerns among ethicists and the experiment itself has inspired numerous business ethics case analyses.

As noted privacy lawyer Daniel Solove (2014) points out, "The problem with obtaining consent in this way is that people often rarely read the privacy policies or terms of use of a website. It is a pure fiction that a person really 'agrees' with a policy such as this, yet we use this fiction all the time."

Personal data and inappropriate business models

The primary problem associated with building a business model around the use of personal data was highlighted by Bloustein more than five decades ago: "...privacy is not to be confused with something of pecuniary value" (Bloustein 1964, p. 162). We have arrived at our present surveillance economy where organizations profit from the exploitation of personal data simply because the legal system in the United States does not specifically protect personal data—a deficiency that Warren & Brandies sought to address in the late 19th century. This lack of protection stems from what James Moor (1985) described as a policy vacuum: "A typical problem in computer ethics arises because there is a policy vacuum about how computer technology should be used. Computers provide us with new capabilities and these in turn give us new choices for action. Often, either no policies for conduct in these situations exist or existing policies seem inadequate." When specific legal guidance is absent, people and organizations tend to act in accord with their own best interests. The resulting economic system that revolves around gathering, sharing, and processing personal information has evolved merely because no one spoke up to defend personal privacy. As philosophers have warned, this practice has great potential to undermine individual dignity and leave all of us exposed to unwanted manipulation.

Consider the information that Google has gathered from our personal interaction with its services. Using the available variety of Google services, we reveal websites visited, queries searched, ads clicked on, people and places tagged, where we work, where we live, what we look like, what our voices sound like, list of our friends and contacts, interactions we have with others, videos we've watched, places we've visited, religious beliefs, political beliefs, health status, our schedules, various passwords, and where we shop just to name a few (Mardisalu 2018). With its recently announced acquisition of Fitbit, Google will have detailed insights concerning our personal levels of daily physical activity.

From this volume of information, Google has uncanny clarity about the kinds of things we think about and which ideologies motivate our actions. In short, Google understands everything that is important to us. This data is enough to understand our levels of education, our personal financial situations, our religious inclinations, our political viewpoints, our sexual orientations, our health, and everything else that *truly* matters to us. This information is also incredibly accurate. While we may actively choose to deceive our friends and family members about certain aspects of our lives, we *never* lie to our search engine. Perhaps most strikingly, Google knows more about us than we might know about ourselves because of the simple fact that Google *never* forgets. As concerning as this may be, it is relatively straight forward to argue that Amazon knows even *more* about us than Google does because Amazon knows the kinds of entertainment that we enjoy (as indicated by streaming music and movies) as well as our specific purchasing habits, including food and other personal items. This provides a wealth of insight that rivals what only our closest friends and family members may know about us. When this information is combined with information from other sources and subject to data analysis tools, the picture of exactly who we are and what we value becomes startlingly clear.

An ever increasing array of smartphone apps that harvest our personal data only intensifies our vulnerabilities. One of the most quickly growing categories of smartphone apps is the fitness tracker. The companies that produce these apps market themselves as the ultimate aid for the health-conscious consumer. Take, for instance, the SweatCoin (https://sweatco.in/) app that converts "your outdoor steps into a currency to spend on cool products and services." All that is necessary to gain access to these "cool products and services" is our location data. The pretext for collecting location data is to count, verify (through the use of yet additional data about us), and rewarded us for our steps. Exploring their user policy (dated 23 May 2018) reveals that personal location-based data will be combined with other data obtained from "payment and delivery services, advertising networks, analytics providers, search information providers, and credit reference agencies..." In addition, SweatCoin's privacy policy indicates that these data assets "may" be transferred to various third parties in order to expand their business. Their webpage indicates that they partner with more than 300 organizations, including health insurance companies and governments across multiple continents.

Consider the level of insight that can be gained from constant recording of GPS data for a student that is completing an undergraduate degree in a small college town. GPS data will reveal the name and location of the school. The admissions profile and cost structure of the school will reveal specific demographic data depending on whether the school is a community college, a state university, or a private university. An understanding of which buildings someone spends time in will reveal the student's major field of study as well as their fraternity or sorority affiliation. If the person frequently spends time in the Dean of Students Office, this might reveal a "problem child" that should perhaps be avoided as a new hire. GPS data also reveals an individual's social circle, where someone eats and shops in town – in short, location data conveys even greater detail concerning specific socio economic status and the kinds of products someone purchases (as confirmed by data SweatCoin will obtain from the aforementioned payment and delivery services). This same data will likely reveal an individual's class year (as identified by frequent visits to the career center or off-campus travel for job interviews) as well as specific eating and sleeping habits, study partners and romantic partners (because their phones are frequently together). If someone also manages to convince their friends to install the SweatCoin app, the resulting data set will become even more accurate and revealing of personal behavior and activities.

While their respective purposes are rather divergent, it is becoming increasingly difficult to distinguish—from a data privacy perspective—the functional difference between the 24/7 location tracking of any smartphone app and a court-mandated ankle bracelet monitor. One is a social status symbol that we gladly spend our money on, the other is a source of social stigma, yet both produce the very same incredibly detailed picture of our daily routines and travels.

Insights from "less sensitive" data

Even the most mundane forms of data gathering can reveal far more about us than many people realize. While many people readily acknowledge the necessity to protect "highly sensitive" information such as health and financial information, those same people are far less likely to be concerned about "less sensitive" data such as photographs, "likes" and dislikes, and purchase information that are frequently associated with social media use (Marwick and Hargittai 2018).

An especially potent example of significant privacy problems that result from the exploitation of "less sensitive" data was revealed in the spring of 2018 when the world learned about Cambridge Analytica and how they obtained data from 87 million Facebook users. It is staggering to note just how easily so much data was obtained. Approximately 270,000 people were paid $1 each to "take a survey" (typically, a personality quiz) through Facebook. Participation in the survey required people to download an app and consent to sharing data about themselves and their social network. Consent occurs by clicking "I Agree" to the terms and conditions upon installing the app. At the time, Facebook permitted third-party app developers to access personal data about the individual that installed the app, that person's friends list, personal details about each friend, and the set of things "liked" by everyone in each person's friend network. As a result, the initial 270,000 people that installed this app served as a gateway to a composite network of approximately 87 million Facebook users from which data was gathered (Glaser 2018a).

Technically, the activities of Facebook and Cambridge Analytica constitute a data breach and initial reports labelled this as a "Facebook hack" suggesting that somehow Cambridge Analytica broke the law and/or violated Facebook's data policy. Neither of these portrayals is accurate, however. This breach occurred without "stealing" anyone's password or "hacking" anyone's account. No actual "break in" happened. All of the data obtained by Cambridge Analytica was the result of following official Facebook data-sharing policies that were in effect at the time. These policies have since been updated.

It is interesting to note the incredibly rich set of personal insights that derive from something as seemingly trivial ("less sensitive") as what Facebook users "like." Sharing data related to "likes" (and other user activity) is part of a philosophy and general mechanism that Facebook refers to as "frictionless sharing" that is designed to incentivize easy sharing of everything that a Facebook user reads (Paul 2011). This type of mechanism automatically gathers the articles and other social media posts that attract a user's attention, paving the way to incredibly detailed amounts of insight as to what motivates people. Ground-breaking research performed by Michal Kosinski *et al.* (2013) demonstrated how Facebook "likes" can be mapped onto what psychologists call the "Big Five" personality traits (also known as an OCEAN score): openness, conscientiousness, extraversion, agreeableness, and neuroticism. Together, these measures provide an incredibly accurate picture of exactly what is important to each of us. Though Kosinski was never affiliated with Cambridge Analytica, his research demonstrated the power of, and opened to door to, using technology and "big data" to make incredibly accurate predictions about people by leveraging a common statistical analysis technique (such as linear regression) that is readily available with just about any statistical software (Grassegger and Krogerus 2017).

In 2012, Kosinski proved that on the basis of an average of 68 Facebook 'likes' by a user, it was possible to predict their skin color (with 95 percent accuracy), their sexual orientation (88 percent accuracy), and their affiliation to the Democratic or Republican party (85 percent). But it didn't stop there. Intelligence, religious affiliation, as well as alcohol, cigarette and drug use, could all be determined. From the data it was even possible to deduce whether someone's parents were divorced.

The strength of their modeling was illustrated by how well it could predict a subject's answers. Kosinski continued to work on the models incessantly: before long, he was able to evaluate a person better than the average work colleague, merely on the basis of ten Facebook 'likes.' Seventy 'likes' were enough to outdo what a person's friends knew, 150 what their parents knew, and 300 'likes' what their partner knew. More 'likes' could even surpass what a person thought they knew about themselves. (Grassegger & Krogerus 2017)

In addition to privacy breaches that result from intentional data sharing activities among organizations as illustrated above, hacking activities reveal still more data about each of us. In their 2019 Cyber Readiness Report, insurance firm Hiscox reported that 61% of organizations across six European nations and the United States suffered data breaches in the past 12 months. This represents a 16-percentage-point increase over the previous year, demonstrating how quickly the threat of data breaches is escalating (Hiscox 2019). This is an important finding in the context of the European Union's General Data Protection Regulation which requires organizations to disclose all data breaches (this law does not currently exist in the United States). The potency of this volume of data being available to any entity is beyond compare as people are simply not equipped to defend against this level of intrusion into their private lives.

Deceptive user policies and digital resignation

According to Draper and Turow (2019), it is no accident that so much personal data ends up in the hands of organizations because society has been very specifically and purposefully manipulated into giving up this personal data.

Two common strategies that companies use to convey a sense of normalcy around consumer surveillance practices as well as to discourage collective action are publishing privacy policies and promoting various transparency initiatives. Both of these broad strategies depend on four specific rhetorical tactics of obfuscation: placation, diversion, jargon, and misnaming. "Placation involves efforts to falsely appease concerns. Diversion refers to efforts to shift individuals' focus away from controversial practices. The use of jargon—terminology that is difficult for those outside a specific group to understand—not only generates confusion, but may frustrate efforts at comprehension. Similarly, misnaming describes efforts to occlude industrial practice through the use of misleading labels" (Draper and Turow 2019, p. 7).

In the SweatCoin example, as well as with nearly every other available smartphone app, the most prominent form of placation is the prominent placement of a privacy policy. Through a national survey conducted between 2003 and 2015, Turow, et al. (2018), discovered that the "majority of Americans believe incorrectly the mere presence of a privacy policy indicates a website will not share information without permission." With this understanding, the impact of simply having a privacy policy serves as a powerful cue to users not to read a privacy policy at all. Diversion is perhaps the most influential of these rhetorical tools for SweatCoin. The fundamental appeal of their app is that users' steps are converted "into a currency to spend on cool products and services." This is a potent diversion that turns people's thinking away from privacy concerns and toward the lure of free gifts such as iPhones, yoga classes, and Apple Watches. As renowned privacy expert Bruce Schneier (2015) points out, "'Free' is a special price, and there has been all sort of psychological research showing that people don't act rationally around it. We overestimate the value of free. We consume more of something than we should when it's free. We pressure others to consume it" (p. 50). Specific concerns are also diluted with the use of phrases like "from time to time," "occasionally," or by simply including the word "may." For example, consider the phrase "From time to time, we may collect … personal information including…" The use of indefinite words goes a long way to soften the impact of data gathering and sharing policies for the few that actually read privacy policies. Jargon is also an effective mechanism that helps to obscure specific actions that might otherwise alarm users. "Further, we may, from time to time, expand or reduce our business which may involve the transfer of certain divisions or assets of our company to other parties, and the data we store and use, where relevant, may be transferred to such third parties." Statements like this essentially open the door to sharing personal data with a variety of third parties, despite overt statements such as

"100% data privacy" or statements such as "We do not sell your data" that are prominently featured on SweatCoin's homepage. Finally, an excellent example of misnaming is the function "Private Browsing" or "Incognito Mode" that is common in web browser software settings. Enabling this feature conveys the impression that details such as user identity, web sites visited, search terms, and other personal data are somehow protected while browsing the web. In reality, all this feature does is delete certain (though, not all) cookie files when the web browser software is closed. These strategies and tactics culminate in what Draper and Turow (2019) call "digital resignation," or the cultivation of the perception that efforts to control privacy on the part of the user are pointless. In short, it is in the best interest of organizations that profit from our personal data that we simply give up caring about our privacy.

Weaponizing personal data

The level of personal insight gathered about each of us is truly startling. The real danger is that too many people don't seem to care about protecting their data, especially if that data falls into that "less sensitive" category. As long as the data gathered does not contain medical or financial details, far too many people resort to the overly simplistic and ill-informed response, "I haven't done anything wrong, therefore I don't have anything to hide." Not only does adopting this perspective incorrectly and narrowly cast privacy merely as a mechanism to hide shameful acts, it's also incredibly dangerous to both the individual and to society.

People who feel they have nothing to hide fail to consider the larger picture of personal vulnerability. The true dangers of exposing our lives is not that our bank accounts will be hacked, but that *society* will be hacked —one person at a time. When everything that is important to us is exposed, it is trivial to create an electronic blueprint of emotional cues that can be used to push people's buttons. When our motivations, our fears, and the very principles that are important to us are known to others, we become profoundly vulnerable to external manipulation, exactly as Wasserstrom warned decades ago. With this level of personal exposure, what we think and how we behave can be altered in ways that are so subtle that we won't notice when it happens.

Let's return to the data on "likes" that Cambridge Analytica gathered through their personality quiz app on Facebook and how it was used during the 2016 presidential election in the United States. With this data in hand, political campaigns were able to craft up to 40,000–50,000 uniquely worded campaign messages *per day* and assess, in real-time thanks to the analytic tools provided by Facebook and Twitter, just how effective each was according to how quickly and how often it was retweeted or liked. This is a targeted marketer's dream scenario. It is also highly likely that this level of personal insight, when combined with data analysis tools, impacted the outcome of the 2016 election. "Cambridge Analytica was also able to use this real-time information to determine which messages were resonating where and then shape [the candidate's] travel schedule around it. So, if there was a spike in clicks on an article about immigration in a county in Pennsylvania or Wisconsin, [the candidate] would go there and give an immigration-focused speech. When you consider how a few thousands votes in a handful of swing states determined the election, this is no small thing" (Illing 2018). The magnitude of these impacts are greatly amplified with the realization that nearly two thirds of all Facebook users get their news from Facebook and nearly two thirds of those people get their news *exclusively* from Facebook (Pew Research Center 2016).

Cambridge Analytica (now defunct) claimed to have influenced over 200 elections around the globe (Glaser 2018b). "We just put information into the bloodstream of the internet, and then, watch it grow, give it a little push every now and again ... like a remote control," said Cambridge Analytica's chief data officer. "It has to happen without anyone thinking..." Political messaging does not need to be accurate or even true. It merely needs to resonate with people (through understanding "likes" and how they map to the Big Five personality traits) and be propagated through social media (using mechanisms of frictionless sharing) in order to influence voters. Ironically, the impact of manipulating people through insights gleaned from "less sensitive" Facebook "likes" for political gain far outweighs the advantages associated with gaining access to "highly sensitive" financial or health-related information. Personal data is now a proven weapon with which to manipulate individual values and ultimately individual behavior.

Perhaps a personal anecdote will help underscore the potency of leveraging "likes" in the context of the Big Five personality traits for political gain. A family friend voted in a presidential election in the United

States for the first time in 2016. She is a nurse that works at a major health care provider and is an avid social media user. Due to all of the data that has been gathered about her social media habits, postings, "likes," tweets, and retweets, there is a very complete account of all of the things that are personally important to her. The state where she resides was a "battleground" state during the 2016 presidential election. Everyone knew this, especially the social media trolls, many of whom have been traced to a variety of foreign nations. She received daily social media messages that specifically targeted *her*: a young mother of three boys working in the health care industry who is struggling to make ends meet to keep the family afloat. She and her husband are succeeding – but like nearly half of the households in the United States (Weber 2018), they are "just barely" succeeding. The constant stream of messages preyed upon her fears that, if elected, Candidate A would introduce new legislation or regulation that would specifically reduce the salary she was earning in the healthcare industry as a means to make affordable health care more widely available to the public. These messages *appeared* to come from other healthcare workers across the country that were facing similar personal challenges and situations. Many hundreds and thousands of these messages arrived daily for months prior to the election. After enough repeated exposure from a seemingly wide variety of sources such as other nurses, medical groups, or nurses unions, she internalized this perceived threat to her family and became deeply concerned. Given the ability of people to hide their identities and physical locations while online, it is exceptionally difficult for the recipient to realize that such an array of messages from seemingly varied sources actually originated with a very small and concentrated source that didn't need to be located within the country at all.

Absolutely desperate not to have her salary reduced by the threat of a "crack down" on the health care industry, she ended up voting for Candidate B instead of her preferred candidate. When she shared this insight with her family after the election, she received a fair amount of push back for her gullibility and flawed decision logic. It took several months for her to actually come to terms with the reality that a president does not have the power or ability to impact the specific contract between her and her employer that determines her salary. While there are certainly tax and collective bargaining implications associated with any change in political leadership, this is not what she was concerned about. Over time, she became *absolutely convinced* that a victory for Candidate A would result in a dramatic and unaffordable reduction in her personal salary. This alone determined her vote. This alone, several months later, made her feel embarrassed and ashamed for how easily she was manipulated by a relentless barrage of fabricated social media posts that encouraged her to cast her vote in favor Candidate B.

Talking with her now, she will readily indicate how she always agreed (and still does) with the overall policies that were championed by Candidate A, but voted for Candidate B solely to protect her income from (fabricated) threats derived from the personal profile built from her social media usage. This manipulation started off with subtle messages that escalated in severity, directness, and frequency. It was all very carefully orchestrated – so much so that she didn't notice while it was going on. It seems unlikely that she was the *only* person to fall victim to such efforts. It seems plausible that her friends at work received the very same set of messages and that these messages became the topic of conversations at work. It seems plausible that many others behaved in a similar fashion. It was difficult for her to realize and subsequently admit that she was nothing more than someone else's marionette to achieve their desired outcome. It was similarly difficult for her to realize that this intrusion into her privacy had systematically stripped away her personal dignity.

Conclusion
Kramer's 2012 experiment with Facebook users' news feeds was a ground breaking illustration of how easily people's moods and subsequent actions can be manipulated with a new type of "remote control." Although the study was somewhat crude in execution, it demonstrated alarming effectiveness and opened a Pandora's box of new digital possibilities. Kosinski *et al.* 2013 work connected Kramer's efforts with long-established psychological research concerning personality traits thus adding extreme precision to Kramer's methodology. Together, these research projects provide a highly detailed roadmap of exactly how easily individuals can be manipulated—one at a time—using seemingly mundane and "less sensitive" personal data that people typically don't care to protect. This data is gathered not only by the obvious technology giants such as Google, Facebook, Amazon, and Twitter, but also by countless smaller

organizations (many of which we are unaware of) that regularly buy, sell, trade, and stockpile our personal data. When the behavioral implications of digital resignation, exemplified by the pervasive yet deeply flawed "I've got nothing to hide" sentiment, are combined with the application of basic data analytic tools and the shield of anonymity offered by the Internet, the result is the most devastatingly powerful stealth weapon of all time: a toolset and instructional booklet that details precisely how to hack people's thoughts and actions without their conscious awareness. If you use social media, the likelihood is high that you are *already a victim*. Now that this weapon has been created, it is trivial to deploy it repeatedly in another domain for any purpose.

Because these digital capabilities are so new, there are no laws to guide or prohibit such actions. The potency of abuses enabled by policy vacuums is precisely what motivated James Moor to write about computer ethics in 1985. Indeed, prominent philosophers have been warning society about the abuses of private information for more than a century. Surreptitious manipulations of our thoughts, feelings, and actions are a clear infringement of our "right to be let alone" that Warren and Brandeis championed so vehemently in 1890. Individual dignity is clearly violated when others interfere with our actions. Philosopher Richard Wasserstrom (1978) issued a compelling warning that without privacy we become targets for manipulation. Edward Bloustein (1964) argued that without privacy, a man is "...less of a man, less of a master over his own destiny, were he without this right" (p. 163) and spoke with poignant clarity: "He who may intrude upon another at will is the master of the other..." (p. 165). Much of this work has been tragically ignored by society.

It is of paramount importance to society that people realize they *do* have something to hide, despite having done nothing wrong. It is essential to our dignity, our freedom, and our democracy that we make every effort to protect our privacy at all times. A sample list of actions that help protect personal privacy can be found in (Appendix 1).

References

Bloustein E. J., 1964, "Privacy as an aspect of human dignity: An answer to Dean Prosser," New York University Law Review **39**(6), pp. 962–1007.

Draper N. A, J. Turow, 2019, "The corporate cultivation of digital resignation," New Media & Society **21**(8), pp. 1–16.

Gage, 2014, Nov 11, "What an uncensored letter to M.L.K. reveals," *The New York Times*, available at https://www.nytimes.com/2014/11/16/magazine/what-an-uncensored-letter-to-mlk-reveals.html

Glaser, 2018a, March 17, "The Cambridge Analytica Scandal Is What Facebook-Powered Election Cheating Looks Like," *Slate*, available at https://slate.com/technology/2018/03/the-cambridge-analytica-scandal-is-what-facebook-powered-election-cheating-looks-like.html

Glaser, 2018b, Mar 19, "The CEO of Cambridge Analytica Was Caught on Video Offering to Meddle in Elections Using Sex Workers and Fake Bribes," *Slate*, available at https://slate.com/technology/2018/03/cambridge-analyticas-ceo-was-caught-by-channel-4-offering-to-meddle-in-elections-using-sex-workers-and-bribes.html

Grassegger H., M. Krogerus, 2017, January 28, "The Data That Turned the World Upside Down," *Vice*, available at https://www.vice.com/en_us/article/mg9vvn/how-our-likes-helped-trump-win

Hill, Kashmir, 2014, June 30, "Facebook Added 'Research' To User Agreement 4 Months After Emotion Manipulation Study," *Forbes*, available at https://www.forbes.com/sites/kashmirhill/2014/06/30/facebook-only-got-permission-to-do-research-on-users-after-emotion-manipulation-study/#37a692e07a62

Hiscox Cyber Readiness Report, 2019, available at https://www.hiscox.co.uk/cyberreadiness

Illing, Sean, 2018, April 4, "Cambridge Analytica, the shady data firm that might be a key Trump-Russia link, explained," *Vox*, available at https://www.vox.com/policy-and-politics/2017/10/16/15657512/cambridge-analytica-mccabe-facebook-aleksandr-kogan-trump-russia

Kosinski, M., D. Stillwell, T. Graepel, 2013, "Private traits and attributes are predictable from digital records of human behavior," Proceedings of the National Academy of Sciences **110**(15), pp. 5802–05. Available at: https://www.pnas.org/content/110/15/5802.short

Kramer, A. I., J. E. Guillory, and J. T. Hancock, 2014, "Experimental evidence of massive-scale emotional contagion through social networks," Proceedings of the National Academy of Sciences of the United States of America **111**(24), pp. 8788–90. Available at https://www.pnas.org/content/111/24/8788.full

Mardisalu, Rob, 2018, What Does Google Know About You: A Complete Guide, available at: https://thebestvpn.com/what-does-google-know-about-you/

Marwick, A., E. Hargittai, 2018, "Nothing to hide, nothing to lose? Incentives and disincentives to sharing information with institutions online," Information, Communication & Society **22**(12), pp. 1697–713.

Moor, J. H., 1985, "What is computer ethics?," Metaphilosophy **16**(4), pp. 266–275.

Paul, Ian, 2011, Sept 26, "Facebook's Frictionless Sharing: A Privacy Guide," *PC World*, available at https://www.pcworld.com/article/240592/facebooks_frictionless_sharing_a_privacy_guide.html

Pew Research Center, 2016, May 26, News Use Across Social Media Platforms 2016. *Pew Research Center Journalism and Media*, available at http://www.journalism.org/2016/05/26/news-use-across-social-media-platforms-2016

Schnrier, Bruce, 2015, Data and Goliath: The Hidden Battles to Collect Your Data and Control Your World. New York, NY:Norton.

Solove Daniel, 2014, June 30, Facebook's Psych Experiment: Consent, Privacy, and Manipulation. *LinkedIn*, available at https://www.linkedin.com/pulse/20140630055215-2259773-the-facebook-psych-experiment-consent-privacy-and-manipulation

Turow, J., M. Hennessy, N. Draper, 2018, "Persistent misperceptions: Americans' misplaced confidence in privacy policies 2003–2015," Journal of Broadcasting and Electronic Media **63**(2), pp. 461–78.

Verma, Inder, 2014, "Editorial Expression of Concern: Experimental evidence of massivescale emotional contagion through social networks," Proceedings of the National Academy of Sciences of the United States of America, available at https://www.pnas.org/content/111/29/10779

Warren, S. D., L. D. Brandeis, 1890, "The right to privacy," Harvard Law Review **4**(5), pp. 193–220.

Wasserstrom, R. A., 1978, "Privacy: some arguments and assumptions," in Richard Bronaugh, ed., Philosophical Law: Authority, Equality, Adjudication, Privacy. Westport, CT: Greenwood Press.

Weber, B. A., 2018, "43% of U.S. households can't afford the basics," *Big Think*, available at: https://bigthink.com/brandon-weber/official-unemployment-rate-is-down-but-nearly-half-cant-afford-basics-like-housing-food

Appendix 1
Simple Actions That Help Protect Personal Data and Enhance Privacy

What follows is a list of simple actions that anyone can take to help protect their privacy. This list is not intended to be exhaustive, though it is intended to show how easy it is to better protect personal data and privacy through a series of small actions.

1. If you have a satellite provider for television viewing, the manufacture probably wants you to plug the satellite receiver into a telephone jack so that it can report your daily viewing/recording habits. If you don't

connect your satellite receiver to a phone line, your data is not reported. If your satellite box instead connects to your household Wi-Fi connection, you have the option of not providing your Wi-Fi password so the connection does not happen. Withholding this data is likely to incur a small additional monthly fee.

2. Similar to above, the typical internet-connect "smart" television will report data on your viewing habits (the "smart" modifier for any electronic device means that it has a computer built into it). Navigating through the menu structure will reveal settings that can help reduce (though may not eliminate entirely) the amount of data gathering that takes place.

3. You don't "need" to have/use a "smart" phone. Sure, it's convenient, but it will also gather and report data from all aspects of your life and interactions with others.

4. If you do use a smart phone, don't enable "location services" for your apps. If you use apps that need location services, enable them when you use them, turn them off otherwise.

5. Don't take "personality quizzes" or other such surveys that you find online ("What fruit are you?"). No matter how entertaining these quizzes are, their ONLY purpose is to gather your personal data – data that can be used to manipulate you as Wasserstrom indicated many years ago. Be especially suspicious of any survey that claims to pay you to answer their questions – this is a sure sign your data is being sold. How else can they afford to pay you?

6. If you have any kind of personal electronics device (smart phone, tablet computer, etc.) you should limit the type of data that you store in it. Never store a social security number, a credit card number, a bank account number, a birthdate, or any kind of password. The data you enter into these devices never stays exclusively in that device. Instead, your data is stored with the organization or elsewhere on the Internet (cloud storage) where it can be hacked, viewed, and misused by others.

7. Never use your fingerprint or facial recognition to unlock any personal electronic device. This, too, is convenient - but these functions provide no legal protection for the contents of your device. Current legal structures uphold the privacy of data on a device that requires a password for entry, but there is no corresponding legal protection for "place

your thumb here" or "look at your device's camera" to unlock the data your device contains.

8. You don't need to have a "rewards card" for every store where you shop. Sure, you get a discount (usually very small), but it also costs you your data and privacy.

9. Use cash instead of debit/credit cards – cash is anonymous. As a side benefit, you'll be less likely to go into debt along the way because you can never spend more cash than is in your pocket.

10. Use different web browsers (at the same time) for different purposes. If you need to sign in to a specific service (such as Google's Gmail) it will record your EVERY click in this browser software (even in different tabs) and tie all of this data to your login identity. Instead, use one web browser for login-based web use, and simultaneously use a different browser for all other web browsing. This provides some measure of insulation between your officially logged behavior, and all of the rest of your web searching and browsing. No sense in handing Google (or any other company) more of your personal data than you really have to.

11. Use anti-virus and anti-malware software – there are a number of good programs that are freely available. One very good program is "Malware Bytes" that comes in both Windows and Mac versions.

12. Never use a password manager! If you put all of your passwords in one service or piece of software and then this service is hacked, all of your accounts will be exposed.

13. Never have your web browser remember your password (or your credit card number) for you. This convenience-based feature is a terrible security risk and will reveal your online accounts to anyone that gains access to your device.

14. Never log in anywhere using your Facebook (or any other social media) account. This is another terrible idea that preys on our desire for convenience and provides Facebook more of your data that they really shouldn't have.

15. Never use the free Wi-Fi connection at the local coffee shop (or airport, or any other place) to do any web surfing where you log into any of your online accounts. These public Wi-Fi access points are rarely encrypted or protected in any manner. You'll end up getting your login credentials stolen.

16. Don't use "the cloud" to backup any of your data. It is both more cost efficient (over time) and more secure to purchase a large external hard drive to maintain your own backups of your important data. Better yet, keep two backup drives: one in the office and one at home. If either building burns down, you'll still have a backup copy of your data. If you don't like the idea of a backup drive laying around that people could find and access, install encryption software to protect the contents of the drive.

17. Don't use social media. It may be hard to imagine, but millions of people led perfectly productive and fulfilling lives before social media appeared.

18. Don't give out data that other people just don't need. For example, a social security number is needed to withhold taxes from a paycheck or issue a line of credit (and a small handful of related legitimate uses). Everyone else that asks for this data gets a string of nine random digits (usually my childhood phone number, plus two extra digits). No one has ever come back to me to tell me there was a problem with the bogus social security number that I provided over the past several decades.

19. Use a search engine like Duck-Duck-Go that doesn't record and sell all of your search history like Google does. Stop giving away data about things that are important to you.

20. Use TOR software for web browsing – it encrypts everything and even hides the origin and destination of your web surfing data. Installing TOR turns your computer into a web server for other TOR traffic, so companies tend to actively discourage this because it increases network traffic. But, if more people used it, the "burden" on those that do use it would be much less.

21. When paying for online purchases, consider using a payment service such as PayPal instead of a credit card. Using a credit card forces you to reveal your account number, the expiration date, and the security code on the back. All of this data gets stored in a database somewhere (where it can be hacked, stolen, and abused) and can be reused at a later date to engage in a secondary transaction that you did not consent to. This data is also subject to bad actors within the organization and hackers that are external to the organization. How many organizations have your credit card data? Do they keep it secure? How do you know it is secure? When a transaction is completed using PayPal, all you get is an email that says

money has been received and (in some cases) a physical mailing address – which is necessary to deliver a purchase. This transaction does not reveal any data (such as an account number) that can be reused for a subsequent transaction.

22. Set your web browser to reject or block web cookies. Some web sites won't function properly when you do this, though you are highly likely to find this same data, service, or product available somewhere else – it just takes me a few seconds more to find it from another source. You could also consider clicking "page 2" at the bottom of your search results to find that product or service elsewhere.

23. Install ad-blocker extensions to your web browser. Sometimes you can use several of them in combination. These ad blockers will actively tell you how many data requests get blocked in real time and evaluate each web site that you visit according to how well it preserves your privacy. Knowledge is power. Ignorance is always problematic...

24. An interesting extension for the Firefox web browser is "LightBeam." It provides a real-time graphic of all entities that are tracking your every online move. Note that tracking your online activity is not dependent on using one browser or another. All of your online activity is always tracked – this extension just shows you how extensively it happens.

25. On an IBM-type personal computer, you can go one step further and "write-protect" the directory where your web browser wants to store cookie files even if you've told it not to do so. Cookie files cannot be written to a directory that does not allow files to be written there.

26. Enable "incognito" or "private browsing mode" as this will delete cookies each time you close your browser. As discussed previously, this function does not allow you to surf the web anonymously – this function suffers from "misnaming" that suggests it does more than it actually does. But, enabling it will help to prevent unintentional data sharing.

27. When you create online accounts, never use your actual birthday. Do, however, use some date that you can remember next time, if you need to. Bear in mind that your fictitious age will need to be over 18 in order to utilize some online services.

28. Don't click on the "forward this article to a friend" link. Doing so guarantees your friend's email address will be used for more spam messages that are of no interest. Instead, copy the URL yourself and paste it

into a message that you type to that person. Sure, it's an extra step, but one that prevents more unnecessary data sharing.

29. Buy a good, "cross-cut" paper shredder that makes itty-bitty confetti, not one that makes big wide strips that can just be lined up side by side again. Fee ALL old/paid bills and account statements into the shredder instead of just putting them in the garbage. Make sure you put paper into the shredder with the proper orientation so that the words in each line are cut into the maximum number of pieces. Shredded paper can also be recycled.

30. Never click on a link in an email message that asks you to log in to "verify your account" or any such similar activity, no matter how legitimate it appears to be. This is surely a scam and you'll just get your login credentials stolen. If you receive a message from your online account provider with this type of message, open a web browser and type their web address yourself to log into your account and check for problems.

31. Have you ever handed your credit card to a total stranger and then let them walk away, out of sight, for 10 minutes? This happens every time you go to a restaurant. If you pay with your credit card, use the kiosk on the table instead. Better yet, pay with cash.

32. Don't send your DNA to 23andMe.com or any other such service. This just exposes your entire family to potential abuse of your genetic profile. This data, unlike a password, cannot be changed once it is exposed. It is one thing to expose your own data (because you consented and "opted in" to such activity), but submitting genetic data automatically opts-in for your entire extended family (even your unborn children) without ever seeking their consent.

33. The bottom line for online services: "If it's free, you're the product."

CROSSCURRENTS

THE SURVEILLANCE OF THE VICTIM
Visibility, Privacy and the Crisis of Bodies in Franciscan Thought

David B. Couturier

We live in an "age of accelerations," where the volume and velocity of change impact and affect every sector of our lives (personal, social, cultural, psychological and spiritual). No arena of our lives has proliferated as quickly or as thoroughly as the widespread collection and often re-sale of personal information by government and law enforcement agencies, global social media corporations, retail and e-commerce digital platforms, mobile telecommunications and smart infrastructure systems. We are constantly being surveilled and vast amounts of data about us are being abstracted, collected, digested, analyzed, reconfigured and processed through algorithms to determine our preferences, beliefs, hopes, and commercializable desires. David Lyon has defined surveillance as "any systematic and routine attention to personal details, whether specific or aggregate for a defined purpose. That purpose, the intention of the surveillance practice, may be to protect, understand, care for, ensure entitlement, control, manage or influence individuals or groups" (Lyon 2018: 3).

We are surveilled by military intelligence, government administrations, at work, for crime control and our consumer activity. Our bodies are being scanned, monitored and evaluated at airports and on street corners, and our biometric details in the form of facial recognition, iris and fingerprint patterns are increasingly being sought by states, corporations, institutions, medical agencies, and insurance companies for a host of reasons, both benign and troubling. Rationales of terrorist threat and border infiltration by the criminal 'other' have intensified the call for increased security and scrutiny. This rapid acceleration and assemblage of personal data has up until now outpaced theological evaluation. In this article, we will outline the scope of the surveillance situation we face and are likely to confront in the near future. We will then speak about the limits of our present implied "theology of privacy" as an adequate remediation to the social justice issues now arising. Then, we will offer Francis of Assisi's "embrace of the leper" as a potential contribution to the dialogue just beginning on a "theology of surveillance." We focus on the surveillance of the victim because it is the victim of abuse that is most at risk of being silenced, ignored, diminished and made 'invisible' as non-persons even by churches committed to the providential surveillance of a liberating God (Couturier 2019).

Surveillance and data analytics

In its annual report of how much data is collected each minute across the globe, cloud software firm DOMO details the exploding amount of information collected about us: "The world's internet population is growing significantly year-over-year. As of January 2019, the internet reaches 56.1% of the world's population and now represents 4.39 billion people—a 9% increase from January 2018."[1] As Nicole Martin, an expert on AI and big data indicates, Americans are producing and giving up vast (and permanent) amounts of information about themselves (without compensation) every minute of the day:

> Overall, Americans use 4,416,720 GB of internet data including 188,000,000 emails, 18,100,000 texts and 4,497,420 Google searches every single minute.
>
> We communicate through our phones more than just by calling. Along with the millions of texts and emails sent each minute, Skype users make 231,840 calls and people are tweeting out their thoughts at 511,200 tweets a minute.
>
> App downloads are on the rise with 390,030 a minute. There are millions of apps now available to do pretty much anything you can think of. You can post photos to Instagram (277,777 stories per minute) or send funny gifs to friends (4,800,000 gifs per minute.)

> You can even find yourself a soulmate, or maybe just a date, with Tinder swipes at 1,400,000 a minute.[2]

Our preferences, choices, beliefs, and desires are then being marked, scrutinized, evaluated and analyzed for their commercial value and competitive advantage. They are being used and/or sold on the open and ever rapidly growing personal data marketplace for advertising, strategic marketing and customer management purposes (Cinnamon 2017). Our personal data is not simply being accumulated in some anonymous repository in the cloud to be processed invisibly and without trace-marks. Data brokers now work under the principle that "every actor, event and transaction can be made visible and calculable" (Cinnamon 2017: 610). Data handlers are working to see that our personal data is reassembled and re-interpreted by "unexpected and illegible mechanisms of extraction and control that exile persons from their own behavior" (Zuboff 2015: 85). Data thus collected and re-assembled may be foreign to our own original intent but serviceable nonetheless to the ever-widening commercial interests of those who now own our data. This means that we are exposing enormous amounts of data about ourselves and allowing the new digital power-centers who own the data to interpret our preferences and desires in ways they see fit. We allow them to sell our beliefs, preferences and desires to all sorts of other data brokers without sufficient forms of regulation. This is so because so many of us misunderstand the dynamics of data storage and utilization in a globalized and digitalized economy. As Zuboff (2016) notes:

> We've entered virgin territory here. The assault on behavioral data is so sweeping that it can no longer be circumscribed by the concept of privacy and its contests. This is a different kind of challenge now, one that threatens the existential and political canon of the modern liberal order defined by principles of self-determination that have been centuries, even millennia, in the making. I am thinking of matters that include, but are not limited to, the sanctity of the individual and the ideals of social equality; the development of identity, autonomy, and moral reasoning; the integrity of contract, the freedom that accrues to the making and fulfilling of promises; norms and rules of collective agreement; the functions of

market democracy; the political integrity of societies; and the future of democratic sovereignty.

Privacy regulations once famously and simply articulated ethically by Warren and Brandeis (1890) as "the right to be left alone" appear to be inadequate under the commercial and communication conditions in which we now live. Personal data is divorced from the people who produce it. We tolerate its free-lance usage by corporations who acquire it. This leads to two forms of injustice, as Cinnamon argues: first, it leads to sociocultural misrecognition "which occurs when personal data are algorithmically processed and subject to categorization" and second, it allows for "political misrepresentation which renders people democratically voiceless, unable to challenge misuses of their data" (Cinnamon 2017: 609). Data that is assembled about us and then re-assembled according to algorithmic processes designed to "predict" future acts, events, and so-called potential risky behavior based on inaccurate, insufficient, ideologically-bent or biased classifications can easily lead to false or misleading representations of our bodies and personalities, outside of our scrutiny or control. The following example from Stoddart is instructive (Stoddart 2019):

Data accumulated about us can now be financially "scored" from multiple sources with criteria that have little or no relevance to our credit worthiness. Multiple data sets from various sources can now be re-assembled to socially categorize people according to their so-called "predicted future behaviors," in ways that are unknown and even unavailable to those being scrutinized. These anonymous sorting and filtering processes lead to the placement of persons in specific social personality categories. Furthermore. these new scoring systems are being utilized to judge worthiness to secure loans, mortgages, jobs or health insurance. These scoring procedures are troubling because they are developed with factors or criteria that have no direct or evident bearing on financial capacity (Cinnamon 2017:616). Already, it has been shown that governments will soon have and will begin utilizing just such a personal score about their citizens with data that includes not just their financial standing but also whatever other factors the state wishes to use to control, oversee, monitor or judge their population. Citizens will be scored for factors including individual political activities, driving record, job evaluations, 'positive' economic and moral behaviors that ensure such things as trustworthiness and sincerity and any other actions, attitudes and behaviors deemed "credit worthy" and consistent with government values (Cinnamon 2017: 616–617).

Surveillance of the victims: a theological formulation

Already theologians are producing theological works on surveillance that show the inadequacy of old "theologies of privacy." Augustine's ancient theology of the fragile but private self is one that relies on the development of an "integral personhood" over against the manipulative communications of the state (Dodaro 2004). New theologies of privacy must contend with the fact that an "integral personhood" is endangered when states and corporations are allowed to manipulate ordinary and accepted values and rights, whenever surveillance needs and the threat of terrorism are under consideration. (Barocas and Nissenbaum 2014). The work of Eric Stoddart in this regard (2019, 2014, 2018) is eminently instructive and we rely on his groundbreaking work here.

Stoddart uses the Church's own history of surveillance to instruct us on pathways forward. He reminds us that Christ himself lived a life under surveillance. We know that his birth was announced by angels but was immediately tracked by a Roman census of all the citizens of Israel who had to be accounted for in their cities of origin. We also know of Herod's extensive spy network that tried unsuccessfully to engage the Magi from the East in his web of surveillance, at the time of Jesus' birth (Matthew 2: 1–12). Later Christ's entire prophetic work was under the surveillance of the Roman authorities and the spies from the High Priest's camp for Jesus' failure to uphold the ritual purity of his disciples and his provocative table fellowship with the unclean of Israel. Christ's entire ministry was under the distrustful eye of Rome's brutal occupying forces in Israel. The Roman and High Priest surveillance apparatus operated because the entire Jewish nation was in the mood for violent rebellion. It suspected that this was Jesus' ultimate messianic strategy as well. In fact, however, Jesus rejected violent rebellion as counterproductive, since, as he said, "those who live by the sword, die by the sword" (Matthew 26:52). Nonetheless, Jesus is accused of fomenting treason by those who charge him with state insurrection and religious heresy. And their paranoid surveillance system goes after him and finds him in the Garden of Gethsemane.

Stoddart offers that the Church will only understand the dangers of surveillance (its own and those of states and corporations) when it reflects on the Christ who surveils and the way in which he does so. We learn much when we remember that Jesus lives in a thick surveillance culture and has to navigate its social, cultural, military and religious traps. Stoddart states baldly: "Christ is one who surveils." (Stoddart 2019). Unlike his religious and political contemporaries, Jesus' gaze is one of compassion and tenderness. It is benevolent and liberating. Christ's surveillance strategies are different from those of "that fox Herod" (Luke 13:32). He is the one who watches over his own and goes in search of the prodigal ones and the sheep who are lost. His is a providential watchful care for the widow and orphan, the unrighteous and unclean.

There is another way to portray Christ's surveillance, that is *from the Cross* (Stoddart 2019). Christ's cruciformed model of surveillance contradicts and critiques the dictatorial forms of surveillance we find within the Gospel stories. The Christic surveillance demonstrates Jesus' solidarity with all those who have been under unjust surveillance and condemned, as He was. We learn about our own "theologies of surveillance," by reflecting on the significant surveillance measures taken against Jesus by the imperial and religious forces of his day. These reflections have the potential to activate the Church to the dangers of surveillance in our own day. And more, they open up the dynamic of invisibility always at play when surveillance measures become opaque or distorted (Stoddart 2019). That is, a theological analysis of surveillance in the life and times of Christ allows us to analyze and understand the ways that surveillance measures try to own and operate our visibility and invisibility in society, how we make ourselves known and present in the social order. The question is not simply whether we are public or private anymore, but how and whether we stand visibly or invisibly in the public square, with or without our permission. We learn that it matters how our personhood is distorted or not and what we would do to protect the way we "come and go," make ourselves known or unknown in the public square of life, and how our presence there is distorted or not.

In Jesus' case, the distortion created by political and religious authorities is both significant and severe. His surveillance by the Roman imperial forces for political terror leads him to become not just the unacceptable "Other," but, more tragically, the "non-person." It is his sentencing to the cross for treason and heresy, based on religious misrecognition and political misrepresentation and the convenient lies at his trial, that leads to his being virtually-dead as a condemned criminal under the Law. The intent of condemnation, conviction and crucifixion is to make Jesus only *visible enough* so as to be soon forgotten, de-memorialized, and as "among the dead and long forgotten" (Psalm 88:5).

This issue is critical. Jesus' trial is held in secret, during the dead of night. The axis on which he is tried is not that of the public-private. The very designation as a convicted criminal sentenced to death by crucifixion under the Law changes the social category by which Jesus is seen and is to be judged by the people. He is already "among the dead." The axis on which his death and dying are to be understood is "visibility" and "invisibility." The Roman forces use crucifixion so that Jesus is seen, understood and rejected as a threat to the nation. He is made visible on the Cross as a criminal guilty of treason and sedition. The mechanics of social and cultural visibility and invisibility are political in nature. Rome believes it is in control of the visible and invisible. Making a show of Christ's torture and death is a temporizing of Christ's visibility so as to control Christ's ultimate social invisibility. Christ's crucifixion is meant by the Empire to accelerate his eventual and ultimate political invisibility. However, the Gospel relates a different dynamic.

At his condemnation, Jesus takes charge of his visibility and invisibility. He does not leave his visibility for others to manipulate. Christ's surveillance from the Cross takes up and owns the invisibility imposed upon him by the state. He hangs in solidarity with all those before and after him who have been unjustly surveilled, scrutinized, and socially categorized and misrepresented, those the authorities thought that "it is better that one man die than the whole nation be lost" (John 11:50).

I have argued elsewhere that the social category that Jesus adopts on the Cross is that of victim in solidarity with all of the victims of history (Couturier 2019). Jesus takes upon himself the ancient tragedy that befell his people as victims in the brickyards of Egypt, where they labored as slaves and as "nonpersons" under the degrading eye of Pharaoh and his enforcers. In his resurrection, Jesus subverts the "invisibility" that surveillance imposed him and becomes "hyper-visible," the ultimate sign that contradicts the superb violence of his age. He reshuffles the facts and aligns them in their truthful biblical order, as Jesus reminds his disciples about the Scripture's foretelling of him, as he walks with them on the road to Emmaus (Luke 24:13–35).

As we have seen, one of the dangers of an indiscriminate surveillance culture is the denial of legitimate visibility that attends when people are separated from their own personal data and they are re-described according to algorithms of anonymous assemblage. Data collection is the performance to find the acceptable bodies, the conformable bodies, and the adjustable bodies who fit the inscrutable and non-democratic criteria being constructed in anonymous and adjustable social categories.

In his resurrection, it is Christ who owns his visibility and takes it up again ("no one takes my life from me" John 10:18). In the Resurrection, Christ owns his hyper-visibility as the Crucified and Risen One: he appears at will, through locked doors, eating and drinking in the early morning hours, to select disciples and to the five-hundred, and then rising into the clouds. The person-as-person who disappeared into the darkness of the non-person of that long and tragic Good Friday afternoon reappears as the crucified and risen One. The algorithm of perfection is rejected in the Resurrection, for Christ returns simultaneously glorified and crucified, thus aligning himself with all those who have failed and been rejected. In his resurrection, Christ is made "hyper-visible." The Letter to the Colossians, written about twenty years after his death and resurrection will remind us that he is "the image of the invisible God, the first born of all creation," and that "all were created through him; all were created for him. He is before all else that is" (Colossians 1: 15–20).

The surveillance of Christ from the Cross is forgiving and reconciling. His surveillance creates community, not tribes. His cruciformed surveillance provides the poor with perspectives on how to subvert every surveillance of oppression, by upending the logic of imperial regimes and "bringing up the lowly" (Luke 1: 46–55). It attends especially to those who have been ejected from society and re-establishes them into the kingdom of God, "this day you will be with me in paradise" (Luke 23:43). Those who have been alienated are brought forward and their names are "inscribed in the book of life" (Revelations 20:15). Their data is stored "in spirit and in truth" (John 4:24).

The surveillance of the leper

Irma van der Ploeg has written a fascinating work on the changed meaning of the human body in our post-modern culture of surveillance. She argues that when the human body is the direct object of surveillance, it changes in meaning, for it has now been made "machine readable." The "scannable body" becomes more than a collection point of data and information. What is developed is a new body ontology (van der Ploeg 2003: 67). The body that is scannable is perceived, understood, received and respected (or not) in new and different ways. The scannable body is now the "informational body," to be used for data retrieval, information bits that can be collected, stored, reassembled, categorized and resold.

Van der Ploeg traces this history of body ontologies and we summarize it briefly here. In the 19th century, for example, we understood ourselves as inhabiting the "anatomical-physiological body." In the early 20th century, this ontology of the body was revised to fit our scientific discoveries of the human body as a biochemical entity made up of chemical substances involved in various feedback loops of messaging and signaling. We knew ourselves, she indicates, as *endocrinological bodies*. The HIV-AIDS crisis of the 1980s forced a new ontology, the acknowledgement of the *immunological body*, whose cells were battling one another in a kind of cellular warfare. And now in the 21st century, as noted above, we are constructing a new ontology, one focused on the *informational body* that produces facts, data and information about us. This factual rendering of our bodies can easily lose touch with us as persons, beings beyond material description. What is revealed is that surveillance procedures now allow governments, corporations and other entities to have information about us, but they lack relational knowledge about us. As Rachel Muers reminds us, God has *knowledge* of us and not simply *information* about us. God's knowledge of us is *relational, not informational* (Muers 2004). This may be what Dr. Eric Topol is getting at, in his study of *Deep Medicine*, when he speaks about the retrieval and medical necessity of deep empathy in the age of artificial intelligence (Topol 2019). With the advent of artificial intelligence in medicine and the supernova capability of computers to digest and analyze millions of bits of information about us, we want our physicians to know something more about us than information.

We expect them to have a relational knowledge of who we are as sick and disabled persons.

We remind ourselves that the conversion of St. Francis of Assisi began as a "crisis over bodies," as well. We learn that Francis could not go within two miles of a leper hospice without demonstrating his disgust and disdain for bodies disabled from leprosy or Hanson's Disease. Francis had grown up a child of privilege, the son of a wealthy cloth merchant. His ambitions as an adolescent were of fame and fortune and to fight for the good and glory of his beloved town of Assisi. Francis had an exalted view of himself and his destiny; his instincts were that he was made for greatness. He went to war to realize it.

He came back from war disillusioned and broken in body, mind and spirit. He had seen his childhood friends, the ones he used to party with, massacred and left for dead on the bloody floor of the Umbrian Valley. His disillusionment and despair were sub-total. He couldn't believe that his family, his society and his church had allowed him to go to war and possibly death to advance their and his own lust for violence and greed. He returned to Assisi after his incarceration as a prisoner of war to search for a new path and purpose for his life. For a while he retained his disdain and disgust for lepers and maintained his distance from them. That distance, however, was not just in meters or miles. The dislocation between him and lepers was a political, religious, social and psychological distance. The distance had cultural and religious meaning of extraction and exclusion (Couturier 2017).

It would not have been uncommon for Francis to have participated in some way in the religious ritual that banished lepers from Assisi. The bishop would gather those found to be with leprosy of whatever age, sex, class or social standing. Prayers would be said and tears shed, as the ritual came to its crescendo with a shovel and dirt thrown on the lepers, mimicking a graveside internment, to be followed by a prayer for the dead. The leper would become by church command no more than the living dead, those forever excluded from the companionship and comradery of civilization. They would be blessed and extracted from society, forevermore at the mercy of the wilds. The leper would have been officially made "invisible" to humankind, unworthy of attention, reduced to non-personhood for the rest of their lives in the wild forests in the valley below Assisi. They were obligated to announce their limited and distant visibility by the rattle of sticks, so that others could depart from their path.

The rattles assured that the lepers were surveilled by society; their movements were monitored by authorities and subjects alike. Their social classification had been changed by the public and visible act of the "*separatio leprosorum*," by which the individual was ritually buried by the community, exiled to the edge of the settlement and then subsequently shunned by society at large as a person no longer.

When Francis embraces the leper on the road, he reverses the dynamics of visibility and invisibility. He turns his disgust into dignity and makes the leper visible again, indeed even central to the whole meaning of his religious Franciscan movement. One might say that the leper becomes "hyper-visible" as Francis moves the entire episode and his own religious call from hostility to hospitality. Francis replaces surveillance with service, as he turns a providential eye of care and compassion on the leper who joins (or, one might say, leads Francis into) a movement where the entire creation becomes a brother-sisterhood of hospitality. The crisis over bodies which coincided with Francis' threats of terror and fears of insecurity is re-engineered and the ontology of bodies from which Francis worked, the ontology of the diseased and distanced body of the leper, becomes re-narrated as the ontology of the *body of a brother resurrected* to personhood in the graced fraternity of the lesser brothers.

Just as Christ's body was crushed and broken to make it invisible and socially useless by the political and religious leaders of his day, so too is Francis' body weakened by the ravages of war, malaria and leprosy. When Francis returns to LaVerna at the end of his life, he is convinced that the ontology of his own body has been found wanting and useless, as good for nothing. His body is wracked by sickness, disease and the results of his enormous penances. However, all seems for naught. Francis is disillusioned and convinced that he has lost control of the religious movement he had begun. He comes to Mount LaVerna in deep distress. However, the Stigmata, the imprinting of Christ's nailmarks on Francis' body, makes his body hyper-visible as the means by which his fraternity will be recognized and reformed. The Stigmata also reveals that the negative surveillance of the brothers will be transformed. The mockery and murmuring against Francis, the brother who knocks at the friary door at midnight and is rejected by his own fraternity, will be recast not as rejection but as a "perfect joy," the moment of fraternal reconciliation.

The surveillance of the lepers created social, religious, cultural, and political distance. The surveillance of Francis by the brothers created distance, distress and distrust, so much so that Francis became convinced that he had failed in what God had given him to do as "the little one" and "minister" of his brothers. However, the Stigmata at LaVerna brought clarity, meaning and purpose. Francis emerged from the shadows of rejection with the markings of the Crucified, participating in the new cruciformed and providential surveillance of all creation that "brings near all who are far off" (Ephesians 2:13). It replaces misery and mayhem with mercy. All classifications are realigned to compassion and forgiveness. Cruciformity is, in essence, having our lives conformed to the crucified Christ. Michael J. Gorman offers that *"(t)he cross is the interpretive, or hermeneutical, lens through which God is seen; it is the means of grace by which God is known."* (Gorman 2001, 17).

All of this happens by an ethic beyond privacy with its negating habit of "leave me alone." The surveillance of privacy once guarded by the taxonomy of distortion, invasion, exclusion, aggregation (Solove 2006) reveals itself as once again (ethically) limited since it presumes specific individuals making individual choices and decisions. The reality is that the process has become cloaked in anonymous and mechanized processes, as Stoddart and Yngvesson (2018, 40) maintains: "We are categorized and assigned to virtual groups on the basis of datafields- the setting up of which are profoundly political and non-innocent acts. Existing biases and prejudices are coded with outcome of material advantage and disadvantage for actual people."

What Francis learns at LaVerna are the lessons of a new surveillance created in fraternal dialogue. Up until now, the friars have been watching Francis with increasing levels of mistrust and frustration. He, for his part, has been surveilling the brothers with his own depressing modes of disappointment. By the end of his life they had arrived at a stalemate of mutual dissatisfaction and dis-ease. However, it is Francis' stigmatized body that will re-narrate the meaning of mercy and compassion. The body sacrificed for the other, the body that does the work of mercy, however spent, is the means of reconciliation and the font of peace. Francis' body upends the social norms ordinarily used to categorize goodness, happiness, joy and blessedness. He once again learns through the gaze of the Seraph that it is the poor and crucified One who sees correctly, measures rightly, judges mercifully and blesses fairly. It is Christ's surveillance from the Cross, repeated on Mt. LaVerna and inscribed on Francis' body that realigns the data of saving grace, where the last shall be first and the first last (Luke 13:30).

Conclusion

We live in an age where the supernova capability of our computers can make certain people socially visible and others politically invisible according to the epiphenomenal categorization and ubiquitous methods of social sorting and filtering achieved by our surveillance industries. Our experience already reveals that these processes are neither benign nor rare.

Theology allows us to review these procedures and provides scriptures and stories that allow us to go beyond abstract discussions of privacy rights that, in the end, merely "leave us alone." We need a new and more vibrant social ethic. What Franciscan theology provides is an instance of cruciformed surveillance in the life of Francis of Assisi that dramatizes how, in an age of data-driven social categorization, we learn to own and act out our visibility and invisibility in the public square and in the digitized world and cloud as sisters and brothers for the sake of victims.

Notes

1. DOMO, "Data Never Sleeps, 7.0) accessed at: https://www.domo.com/learn/data-never-sleeps-7
2. Nicole Martin, "How much data is collected every minute of the day," *Forbes* (August 7, 2019), accessed at: https://www.forbes.com/sites/nicolemartin1/2019/08/07/how-much-data-is-collected-every-minute-of-the-day/#8b7cfda3d66f

Works Cited

Gorman, Michael J., 2001, Cruciformity: Paul's Narrative Spirituality of the Cross. Grand Rapids, MI: Wm. B. Eerdmans.

Muers, Rachel, 2004, Keeping God's Silence: Towards a Theological Ethics of Communication. Oxford: Blackwell.

Topol, Eric, 2019, Deep Medicine: How Artificial Intelligence can Make Healthcare Human Again. New York: Basics Books.

Couturier, David B., 2019, The Voice of Victims. The Voice of the Crucified, St. Bonaventure, NY: Franciscan University Publications.

Barocas, Salon, and Helen Nissenbaum, 2014, "Big Data's End Run around Anonymity and Consent," in J. Lane, V. Stodden, S. Bender, and H. Nissenbaum, eds., Privacy: Big Data and the Public Good: Frameworks for Engagement, New York, NY: Cambridge University Press, pp. 44–75.

Cinnamon, Jonathan, 2017, "Social Injustice and Surveillance Capitalism," Surveillance and Society **15**(5), pp. 9–625.

Couturier, David B., 2017, "From an Economy of Extraction to an Economy of Inclusion," Franciscan Connections: The Cord **67**(3), pp. 26–33.

Dodaro, Robert, 2004, Christ and the Just Society in the Thought of Augustine. Cambridge, UK: Cambridge University Press.

Lyon, David, 2018, "God's Eye: A Reason for Hope," Surveillance and Society **16**(4), pp. 546–53.

van der Ploeg, Irma, 2003, "Biometrics and Privacy. A Note on the Politics of Theorizing Technology," Information, Communication, Society **16**(1), pp. 85–104.

Solove, Daniel J., 2006, "A Taxonomy of Privacy," University of Pennsylvania Law Review **154**(3), pp. 477–560.

Stoddart, Eric, 2014, "(In)visibility Before Privacy: A Theological Ethics of Surveillance as Social Sorting," Studies in Christian Ethics **27**(1), pp. 33–9.

Stoddart, Eric, Susanne Wigorts Yngevesson, 2018, "Surveillance and Religion," Surveillance and Society **16**(4), pp. 393–98.

Stoddart, Eric, 2019, "Reforming Bodies Under Surveillance: an urgent task for theological education," in A. Vahakangas, S. Angel, and K. Helboe, eds., Reforming Practical Theology: The Politics of Body and Space, IAPT.CS 1: pp. 176–183. https://doi.org/10.25785/iapt.cs.v1i0.73

Zuboff, Soshana, 2015, "Big other: surveillance capitalism and the prospects of an information civilization," Journal of Information Technology **30**(1), pp. 75–89.

Zuboff, Soshana, 2016, "The Secrets of Surveillance Capitalism," Frankfurter Allegmaine Zeitung. Accessed at: httsp://www.faz.net/aktuell/feuilleton/debatten/the-digital-debate/shoshaa-zuboff-secrets-of-surveillance-capitalism-14103616.html

CROSSCURRENTS

WHISPERS IN THE CLOSET
Reflections on TSA and Solitude

Taraneh R. Wilkinson

Privacy is not the same as solitude. Privacy involves a composite set of legal definitions and, as a distinct civil right, lacks definite consensus. Solitude, like privacy, can be a vague term, but it also tags additional theological and spiritual dimensions. As the rhythms of cities and lives change to reflect an increasing population and a growing penetration of technologies into our most intimate realms, it is safe to say that both access to privacy and solitude may be at risk. Yet, privacy can come at the cost of convenience or even safety. How, then, do we adjudicate between the benefits of privacy and security in today's uncertain world?

TSA-induced reflections on privacy

In the American context, the legal and social understanding of privacy has evolved over time and remains a territory of constant negotiation. One space where this ongoing negotiation has been highly visible is that of airport security checkpoints. Founded in 2001 shortly after the 9/11 terrorist attacks, the Transportation Security Administration, an agency of the U.S. Department of Homeland Security, represents the American choice to prioritize security over privacy at the airport and other places of public travel. However, with new technologies and changing political climates, the trade-off between security and privacy has not been static. Whether it be the now obsolete back scanners that produced near-naked images of passengers or the DHS (paid) Global Entry program, various new protocols have come into place over the years that renegotiate the line between security and privacy for airport travelers. Sometimes, as in the case with the back scanners in 2013, Americans may consider a line of privacy crossed that is not justified by the projected gains in security.[1.]

Take for instance the present increase in additional security screening. Since at least 2016, some passengers have been subject to non-random extra security screening as part of the TSA Secure Flight Program, first implemented in 2009. At the time of writing this article, it has become common for many frequent fliers to obtain a Redress Control Number from the Department of Homeland Security to avoid this non-random extra security screening at airports.

As an illustration, I offer my own encounter with this extra screening. Like most air-fairing travelers, I do not look forward to security checks—socks on cold, public floors, awkwardly juggling toiletries, human bottlenecks, or extra x-rays are usually not crowd-pleasers. While passing through security checkpoints, a microcosm of our so-called modern age, individuals are reduced to numbers and mechanical procedures. Privacy is momentarily forfeited for the greater good, and indeed privilege, of discovering and connecting with the world. Normally, I accept this trade-off without much thought.

However, in August 2019, while preparing for a domestic flight, I found I could no longer check in online. At the check-in counter my boarding card had a large "SSSS" written in the corner. And while I was aware of US citizens being detained and questioned at international border crossings (apparently over 33,000 times in 2018[2.]), I was not aware that the SSSS entailed targeted extra screening for any US flight, domestic or international. The boarding card elicited a conspicuous red flash on the officer's machine at the security checkpoint. They explained to me that I would be subject to special screening and proceeded to take me away from the crowds, scan my luggage separately, open all of it, conduct a chemical swab of external and internal contents, ask me to turn on all my electronic devices for them to see, and give me a thorough and physically invasive pat down.

At the gate, I asked the attendant what the meaning of this extra screening might be. She replied that they must have lowered the threshold for security threat. This left me with a distinct impression that she took for granted that I, or anyone with an SSSS on their boarding pass, was automatically a security threat, even if not of the highest level. I was unnerved that she unquestioningly accepted TSA's treatment of US citizens who have not been subjected to legal summons or due process as suspicious and potentially dangerous. I thought to myself that there was nothing patriotic in happily accepting the government demonizing its citizens in the absence of due process. Rather, I would assume such an attitude to be the very opposite of patriotism, considering rule of law and due process are cherished national values.

On the return flight, again, my boarding card was stamped with an SSSS. I asked the TSA officer whether the extra screening was random. He replied with a firm "No ma'am, it is not random," as I began to wonder what non-random criterion of selection could be at play. TSA's policies are meant to prohibit unlawful profiling based on ethnicity, race, or religion. Had I been singled out for my non-European given name, my travel to Muslim majority countries, or my scholarship on Turkish Muslim thought? After all, TSA Quiet Skies program has recently targeted US-citizens who have traveled to Turkey, despite repeatedly claiming they do not surveil "ordinary citizens."[3] How chilling it is to imagine that even studying Islam or visiting Muslim countries might be enough to raise suspicions or conclude that a US citizen is not ordinary. If ethnic, racial, and religious profiling are legally prohibited, this raises the matter of who is presumed not ordinary and how far the designation "not ordinary" might serve to cover up cases of illegal profiling. In 2017 the American Civil Liberties Union published a study criticizing the TSA Screening Passengers by Observation Techniques program as unscientific racial and religious profiling, implementing pseudo-science as a "license to harass."[4] Evidently the designations of "ordinary" and "not ordinary" have helped obscure situations where an individual's privacy has been unduly violated in the name of security, lacking clear evidence that such a trade-off would be necessary, just, or effective.

In my case, I contacted the Department of Homeland Security via their website and filed an electronic complaint through their Traveler Redress Inquiry Program (TRIP).[5] On my next flight, again, the boarding card read SSSS. My desire to speak up against this potential violation of due process rights conflicted with the consideration that TSA officers hold unquestionable authority at checkpoints. For instance, when Nadine Pellegrino spoke up against TSA harassment in 2006, she was "arrested and charged by the district attorney with 10 crimes, including aggravated assault, possession of an instrument of a crime (her luggage), and making terroristic threats."[6.] Voicing an objection to the process could make things worse. I had to weigh my own concern for privacy against the potential risk to my person in speaking up. While I was in no way pleased to see my personal affects, calendar, and diaries searched through item by item, I drew the line at bodily privacy. I told them that I objected to being touched intimately by a TSA officer, but that I would comply despite my objection. To borrow words from celebrity Brooke Mueller, who was also aggressively touched and handled by the TSA spring 2019, "The invasion of my body was borderline abusive. It's not like they had just cause to treat me like a drug smuggler."[7.]

Privacy: a short history
Such increasingly common intrusive experiences at the hands of TSA render the history of privacy in the United States highly relevant to our present moment. It is no wild exaggeration to suggest that our evolving legal definition of privacy and current technologies often serve as handmaids to government organizations like the TSA, Homeland Security, the FBI, etc. Still, what is privacy exactly? How has it been understood and defined? What is considered a reasonable expectation of privacy in our current information age?

As Judith DeCew explains in the *Stanford Encyclopedia of Philosophy*, debates on privacy include both descriptive accounts of what is protected (discussion of such protections takes on steam in late nineteenth-century legal debates) as well as normative accounts of the value of privacy (taken up in philosophical discussions from the mid-twentieth century onward).[8.] Privacy has since been characterized variously as the ability to control information about oneself, protection from unwanted access, as necessary to human dignity, or crucial for intimacy with other persons; some also view privacy as necessary for peace of mind or important to facilitating self-expression and personal choice.[9.]

Legally speaking, privacy is not explicitly guaranteed in the US Bill of Rights. As a consequence, many definitions of privacy have sought to link privacy to other rights. Constitutional support for the right to privacy is primarily embodied in the Fourth Amendment, which states that "the right of the people to be secure in their persons, houses, papers, and effects, against reasonable searches and seizures, shall not be violated." In addition, the First Amendment names freedoms of speech, religion, and assembly as inviolate, and the Fifth Amendment ensures due process (specifically, no deprivation of life, liberty or property without due process). The Fourteenth Amendment dates to 1868 and forbids states to deny "any person" their "life, liberty, or property" without due process. These, bundled together, have historically served as lynch pins in defining and protecting privacy rights in the United States.

In 1881 Judge Thomas McIntyre Cooley discussed "the right to be let alone."[10] Samuel D. Warren and Louis D. Brandeis's seminal article, "The Right to Privacy," published in 1890 argued for "the right to one's personality," setting forth the principle of "inviolate personality."[11] In the same article Warren and Brandeis expressed their concern that with the advent of an invasive press and new technologies "what is whispered in the closet shall be proclaimed from the housetops."[12] With increasing ability to document private lives through the new technology of photography, Warren and Brandeis were not the only ones concerned to define and defend the right to privacy. In the Supreme Court case *Union Pacific Railway Co. v. Botsford* (1891), Justice Horace Gray declared "no right is held more sacred, or is more carefully guarded, by the common law, than the right of every individual to the possession and control of his own person, free from all restraint or interference of others, unless by clear and unquestionable authority of law."[13]

The capacity for surveillance through developing technologies, such as wire taps, marked Supreme Court discussions starting in the early twentieth century. Despite the *Olmstead* ruling of 1928, the Supreme Court subsequently recognized the importance of leaving broad room for interpreting the right to privacy in adjudicating such cases. *Olmstead v. United States* (1928) ruled for protection of places rather than persons;[14] nevertheless, the dissent Justice Louis Brandeis made a case for "the right to be let alone" calling it "the right most valued by civilized men."[15] Later in *United States v. Lefkowitz* (1932), the Supreme Court ruled for a liberal parsing of the prohibition on unreasonable government search, drawing on The Fourth Amendment to protect the right of privacy.[16] Not long thereafter, 1934 witnessed the Federal Communications Act, or the first law on electronic surveillance. By the mid-late twentieth century, the war on drugs and accelerating technology brought about increasing changes. Even as the Supreme Court in *Griswold v. Connecticut* (1965) declared that the Bill of Rights established a zone of privacy that protected citizens from government intrusions, the 1960s saw law enforcement being given greater power to monitor suspected criminals and criminal activity.

In 1967 *Katz v. United States* reversed the *Olmstead* decision, ruling that officers must have a legal cause to search if a person demonstrates a reasonable "expectation of privacy."[17.] This also shifted the burden of establishing a legal expectation of privacy from government to individual.[18.] Although law enforcement had tapped a phone booth without a warrant, when Charles Katz closed the phone booth door behind him, he signaled that he intended his privacy to be protected. Katz' claim to privacy was upheld. This case inaugurated a two-factor standard in establishing the right to privacy: (1) those subject to surveillance, search, or seizure must believe government intrusion unreasonable and (2) must demonstrate an expectation of privacy by actively protecting their deeds and words from the public eye. The subjective element of the first criterion was later modified: it was no longer sufficient for those subject to surveillance to expect privacy. Instead of hinging the right solely on individual expectations of privacy, society at large had to recognize such expectations of privacy as reasonable. With changing society and times came changing expectations of privacy. This was as much true then as it is now.

Nothing has shaped our expectations of privacy more in the last decades than technology and globalization—with these too appear the specters of amorphous security threats and global terrorism. In this constantly evolving climate, rights to privacy are inevitably weighed against the risks to security, a.k.a. the balancing of competing interests. As William Bloss explains, "In privacy cases, courts determine if government intrusions are valid based upon a determination of the reasonableness of their actions."[19.] Courts currently consider the reasonableness of expectation of privacy and then weigh it against the government's claims concerning public safety.

By the end of the twentieth century, numerous laws had been passed to keep the government abreast of technological change. Notably, in 1994, the Communications Assistance for Law Enforcement Act (CALEA) authorized officials to "locate cellular telephone users, identify callers, or determine telephone features used by patrons."[20.] Although service providers initially resisted, by 2004 providers were required by the FCC to comply with the law. Of course, between the years 1994 and 2004 lies a landmark moment in the evolution of privacy in the United States: 9/11.

The 2001 USA Patriot Act was issued in response to the 9/11 attacks. In a sweeping move to prioritize national security over individual liberty, the act placed new strictures on rights guaranteed by the Fourth and Fifth Amendments. Those who questioned the necessity of suspending individual liberties were met with scathing criticisms like that of Attorney General Ashcroft, who remarked, "to those who scare peace-loving people with phantoms of lost liberty, my message is this: Your tactics only aid terrorists, for they erode our national unity and diminish our resolve. They give ammunition to America's enemies and pause to America's friends."[21.]

Ashcroft was no outlier in prioritizing safety at the possible expense of civil liberties. Pew Research Center surveys, conducted before and after 9/11, have confirmed that when Americans feel security is at risk, they prefer safety over privacy. Shortly after 9/11, a Pew survey reported that 55% of Americans favored sacrificing some civil liberties for the sake of security. Although this number dropped over the subsequent decade, after the San Bernardino and Paris shootings of 2015, again 56% of Americans thought that the government had not gone far enough in fighting terrorism.[22.] Moreover, as many saw with the Facebook scandal that came to a head in March of 2018, both corporations and governments are implicated in the discussion to define and defend privacy. Yet, if social expectations of privacy are diminishing and the legal right to privacy is largely defined on social expectations thereof, what does that mean for the legal future of the right to privacy? Will individual privacy no longer be considered a necessary part of the common good?

Privacy: a condition for human flourishing?
Perhaps privacy should take a back seat to a more basic need like human safety. After all, in Maslow's famous hierarchy of needs safety ranks second only to basic physical necessities like food and shelter. However, it would be premature to say that Americans have always chosen safety above more abstract goods associated with human flourishing and dignity. Indeed, the United States was founded on the notion that independence from Britain outranked the ensuing military repercussions and subsequent risks to life and limb that the revolution cost the young nation. Patrick Henry's famous 1775 speech in Virginia, known by the closing line "Give me liberty or give me death!" immortalized that crucial

historical push to seek the abstract good of freedom even at the risk of life itself. Today the state motto of New Hampshire is still "live free or die." Further, when slavery was a legal component of the US economy prior to 1865, countless enslaved individuals chose to risk everything, including whatever measure of security they might have had, for the promise of freedom. Abolitionists too risked their safety and lives to combat an institution seen as an affront to basic human dignity. Famously, John Brown, was executed in 1859 for leading an anti-slavery raid at Harper's Ferry. In that same vein, civil rights activists in the 1950s and 1960s put their individual safety, communities, and very lives at risk to advocate for a more just and equitable America. A cursory glance at US history shows that safety, while important, does not always take precedence, especially when the question becomes assuring basic human dignity across society at large. There are times when abstract goods such as liberty and human dignity supersede the need for security. The question is whether privacy counts as one of those abstract goods and, if so, when it might overtake security as a priority.

Perhaps "ordinary" citizens have no need to fear the loss of privacy. Still, if privacy consistently plays second fiddle to greater common goods, where does one draw the line? Can the sphere of privacy shrink infinitesimally without negative consequence? Assuming privacy is a necessary component to human dignity and flourishing, the line would ostensibly be drawn where loss of privacy significantly impacts human dignity or the human ability to flourish, so much so that the negative damage outweighs the potential security risks.

In the tech industry, there is talk of the creepy line. The idea is to approach the creepy line but not cross it. The line is not static; it moves over time. What was unheard of thirty years ago is accepted without second thought today. Think of phones that can access our bank accounts, cars that can read our bodies, mail-in kits that tell us our genetic makeup, household appliances that can record and respond to our voice and movements. Some people consider any invasion of privacy justified if it provides ultimate security. Henry Mance cites a computer scientist in charge of a surveillance network, "If we can live in a society where you can walk safely down an alley, I think that creepy line goes away."[23.] For that technician and others, there is no negative consequence to dwindling privacy, because the projected gain of perpetual security far outweighs the sacrifice. This attitude strikes me as naive. It presupposes that those seeking to sow harm can be stopped once and for all with the advent of a surveillance utopia. It blatantly ignores the strong likelihood that the people who do wrong will simply find another way to do wrong, while those who seek to contribute to the common good may find themselves hemmed in by shrinking civil liberties and thus kept from addressing society's needs.

Practically speaking, criminal behavior is not static, it evolves with technology and legal statutes. No one measure will end crime or security threats for all time. But choosing surveillance over privacy might have a threshold of no-return when it comes to our shared civil liberties. These are the questions we must ask ourselves in this age.

In 2002, Patricia Mell declared, "Today's technology has the potential to eliminate the area in which an individual can legitimately declare privacy from the intrusion of the government."[24.] That was before smartphones and Wi-Fi were omnipresent. With the rate of technological advancement nowadays, we are all becoming "known entities."[25.] The mysterious unknown wellspring in each of us is giving way to monitored sleep cycles, heart rates, emotional states, preferences, social interactions, genetic makeup, and biometrics. As our human mystery is brought to light by big data, we are left to ponder where our data goes and who knows or cares to know our most mundane and meaningless habits.

How does privacy contribute to human flourishing? Why might some consider it detrimental for our most intimate details and biological functions to be recorded and analyzed by governmental or corporate entities? For many, privacy may boil down to a matter of basic human dignity. There are parts of our lives and embodied experiences we might not wish to place on public display. There is personal information that we may wish to retain control over. Losing the ability to control and manage the more intimate, i.e. private, details of our lives represents a potential threat to human dignity. Further, maintaining some degree of privacy may be integral to regarding human beings as partially mysterious and free entities. There is a sense in which being a "known entity" risks reducing people to determined and predictable entities, devoid of agency and free will. Even as early as the late nineteenth century, the initial stages of statistical analysis and the budding science of social behavior frightened many with the thought that all human actions could be predicted and classified as parts of describable trends.[26.] In short, not everyone is assuaged at the idea of being a "known entity."

Theologians speak of a vertical or transcendent dimension of the self —a dimension perpendicular to the known plane of existence that puts each of us in contact with the Divine. Solitude can be a tool in accessing and exploring this dimension. Privacy is also arguably endemic to this dimension, for its orientation points beyond the realms of the known, into what it not publicly known or sensed.

Theologian F.D.E. Schleiermacher (1768-1834) believed that the individual self contains elements that transcend the self's constitutive relationships to the rest of the finite existence. In updated terms, the self is something that can never be utterly reduced to a "known entity." In his famous *Soliloques* (1800), he explored the subtle relationship between inner self and outer world, reveling in the intimacy of the inward dimension, a dimension he felt crucial for human freedom. This inward dimension was also a theological dimension, a place where the self transcended time and met the Infinite, or Divine. While the human self may ultimately pose a finite and thus knowable mystery, for Schleiermacher there remains a stubborn sliver, a subtle vector of each individual which stands in solitude from all things finite and knowable. He continued to think of the human self as an entity in intimate relationship to an Infinite that transcended causal and finite factors throughout his life. A passage from his Pentecost Sunday sermon of May 1825 strikes me as a particularly apt illustration:

> If our knowledge of the earth, this particular piece of God's creation given over to us by God, continually expands itself through increased intercourse with all parts of the world; [...] if human dominance is ever more secured over all forces subordinate to it that stir in the world—we may then with the times arrive at a point of saying, with greater right than earlier generations, that the spirit of the world dwelling within us, as the inspirited parts of the world, has searched the depths of the world. And if we were to penetrate even further into the interior of the human spirit, this precious and highest of all earthly powers, and if the mystery of the interconnection of all its inner workings were to be entirely penetrable by us—we would then be able to say that the human

spirit has finally searched its own depths, but these depths are not the depths of the Godhead.[27.]

Even if human beings are ultimately finite, there is a sense in which the plenitude of our relations with the rest of the world is comprised of near infinite depths. Further, even if there were some way to perfect all human knowing and plumb every aspect of our interior and exterior realities, for Schleiermacher, there is at least one dimension of humanity that is inexhaustible: the human relationship with the Divine. The Divine is Infinite and possesses depths that cannot be plumbed, thus ensuring that our relationship to the Divine can never be reduced to something lifeless and determined.

True, it is precarious to found legal definitions of privacy on theological anthropologies which speak only to a section of the population. However, there is still insight to be gained from theological views of the self. By affirming a transcendent dimension to selfhood, one affirms an inviolate dimension of inwardness, akin to many normative accounts of privacy. Affirming that we are not completely knowable as individual subjective consciousnesses is a *de facto* recognition of the ongoing possibility for privacy. It also offers the potential position that the human self is not solely formed in interaction with what is exterior to it, but that it is also formed in relation to itself, in all its openness to Infinity. On a similar note, if we deny that there are parts or dimensions to the self that are co-constituted by access to privacy, we risk damaging or losing those parts of our humanity. I would not like to say exactly *how* necessary those aspects of the self might be to human flourishing.

Homeland conclusions

On Sept 9th, the Department of Homeland Security sent me an impersonal email acknowledging receipt of my complaint. One line caught my eye in particular: "Due to unprecedented volume, it is taking at least 3 months to process cases." What was the cause of such unprecedented volume? How can so many US citizens have been treated as non-ordinary citizens or as threats without any transparency or due process? It looks as though, yet again, the balance between maintaining privacy and security is in dispute.

Recall the two-factor standard for establishing a legal right to privacy in the United States rooted in the 1967 *Katz v. United States* ruling. In order to establish a right to privacy, there must be a personal and societal expectation that a specific government intrusion is unreasonable paired with actions that demonstrate said expectation of privacy. Perhaps by sending in my complaint to Homeland Security I was declaring an expectation of privacy, one thankfully still honored by society and government alike. Early November, I received a snail mail letter from the DHS with my "Redress Control Number." While they can neither confirm nor deny whether I am an ordinary citizen (i.e. whether I am on a watch list or not), at least I can travel again unmolested.

My experience with TSA and Homeland Security is far from uncommon. As David Lindorf notes, "Sixteen years after it was created in the post 9-11 hysteria of the Patriot Act, the Homeland Security Terrorist Watch List is alive and, apparently, going off the rails, with increasing numbers being kept from boarding, while others are simply harassed, seemingly for political activism of one kind or another."[28] In Lindorf's own impersonal correspondence with the FBI the agency wrote, "Nominating a subject to the Terrorist Screening Database (TSDB) cannot be based on race, ethnicity, or religious affiliation; nor on beliefs and activities protected by the First Amendment, such as freedoms of speech, the press, or peaceful assembly. To add a subject to a subset list that prevents an individual from flying or requires secondary screening, a nomination must be received from a U.S. government law enforcement or intelligence agency to meet the reasonable suspicion standard. Mere guesses or hunches, or the reporting of suspicious activity alone are not sufficient."[29] Yet since neither Homeland Security nor the FBI are able to confirm or deny whether those seeking redress are on a list, how do any of us verify or contest the alleged reasonable suspicion that justifies these infringements on our due process liberties?

While I recognize that in practice privacy is often a privilege, I agree with those who argue that some level of privacy should be a right. However, since privacy is so hard to define and its definition so susceptible to shifts in technology, legal rulings, and societal values, it will likely be an ongoing battle to determine and defend the right to privacy. Despite this difficulty, many would agree that privacy is nonetheless necessary for human dignity. The words of the famous Warren and Brandeis article of

1890 may yet resonate with many: "The intensity and complexity of life attendant upon advancing civilization have rendered necessary some retreat from the world, and [...] solitude and privacy have become more essential to the individual...."[30]

Notes

1. TSA removed the invasive backscanners and replaced them with millimeter wave scanners in 2013 amid public backlash over associated health risk and privacy concerns: Daily Mail Reporter, "TSA pulls ALL X-ray body scanners from airports over privacy concerns...but claims they were never a health risk to fliers," *The Daily Mail*, May 30, 2013, https://www.dailymail.co.uk/news/article-2333685/TSA-removes-ALL-backscatter-X-ray-machines-airports-privacy-concerns.html.
2. Seth Harp, "I'm a Journalist but I Didn't Fully Realize the Terrible Power of U.S. Border Officials Until They Violated My Rights and Privacy," *The Intercept*, June 22, 2019, https://theintercept.com/2019/06/22/cbp-border-searches-journalists/.
3. Jana Winter, "Ordinary travelers decry TSA surveillance," *Boston Globe*, August 19, 2018, A.1 (ProQuest).
4. Spencer Ackerman, "TSA screening program risks racial profiling amid shaky science – study," *The Guardian*, February 8, 2017, https://www.theguardian.com/us-news/2017/feb/08/tsa-screening-racial-religious-profiling-aclu-study.
5. Instructions for filing a complaint available on this Department of Homeland Security page: https://www.dhs.gov/how-do-i/file-travel-complaint-dhs-trip (last accessed Dec 5, 2019).
6. "That Abusive TSA Officer" *Los Angeles Times*, September 4, 2019, A.12 (ProQuest).
7. "Touchy TSA Topic," *New York Post*, April 9, 2019, 14 (ProQuest).
8. Judith DeCew, "Privacy," *The Stanford Encyclopedia of Philosophy*, ed. Edward N. Zalta (Spring 2018 Edition), https://plato.stanford.edu/archives/spr2018/entries/privacy/.
9. DeCew, "Privacy."
10. William P. Bloss, *Under a Watchful Eye: Privacy Rights and Criminal Justice* (Santa Barbara: Praeger Publishers, 2009), 5. Cf. Cooley is also cited by Warren and Brandeis. See Warren and Brandeis, "The Right to Privacy," *Harvard Law Review* 4 (1890): 195.
11. Bloss, *Under a Watchful Eye*, 5. Cf. Warren and Brandeis, "The Right to Privacy."
12. Warren and Brandeis, "The Right to Privacy," 195.
13. Bloss, *Under a Watchful Eye*, 5.
14. Bloss, *Under a Watchful Eye*, 7.
15. Bloss, *Under a Watchful Eye*, 4.
16. Bloss, *Under a Watchful Eye*, 3–4.
17. Bloss, *Under a Watchful Eye*, 2.
18. Bloss, *Under a Watchful Eye*, 8.
19. Bloss, *Under a Watchful Eye*, 11.
20. Bloss, *Under a Watchful Eye*, 167.
21. Patricia Mell, "Big Brother at the Door: Balancing National Security with Privacy under the USA Patriot Act," *Denver University Law Review* 80 (2002): 379 ft24. Mell cites Attorney General Ashcroft's testimony before the Senate Judiciary Committee in December 2001, recorded

in Dep't of Justice Oversight: Preserving our Freedoms While Defending Against Terrorism: Hearing Before the Sen. Comm. on the Judiciary, 107th Cong.

22. Shiva Maniam, "Americans Feel the Tensions between Privacy and Security Concerns," *Fact-Tank*, February 19, 2016, https://www.pewresearch.org/fact-tank/2016/02/19/americans-feel-the-tensions-between-privacy-and-security-concerns/.

23. Henry Mance, "Is Privacy Dead?" Financial Times, July 19, 2019, https://www.ft.com/content/c4288d72-a7d0-11e9-984c-fac8325aaa04.

24. Mell, "Big Brother at the Door," 376.

25. Henry Mance, "Is Privacy Dead?"

26. For more on this, see William Barrett's *Irrational Man: A Study in Existential Philosophy* (Doubleday, 1958).

27. Schleiermacher, *Christmas Dialogue, The Second Speech, and Other Selections*, trans. Julia Lamm(New York/Mahwah, NJ: Paulist Press, 2015), 228–229.

28. Dave Lindorf, "Are Terrorism Watch Lists Expanding Under Trump?" *The Nation*, August 22, 2019, https://www.thenation.com/article/trump-terrorism-travel-watchlist/.

29. Ibid.

30. Warren and Brandeis, "The Right to Privacy," 196.

CROSSCURRENTS

PRIVACY AND DIGITAL LIFE
What Do I Owe My Neighbor

Theresa E. Miedema

Part I: Introduction

With the ever-increasing proliferation of technology that is "smart" enough to watch us and gather our data, it is easy to resign ourselves to diminishing spheres of privacy. We are told that our privacy is a small price to pay for the convenience and efficiencies that flow from automating tasks and tracking our data. Some of us have the luxury of shrugging off technical intrusions in our lives: we are not among those who are hyper-surveilled or who are at risk for mis-identification by law enforcement. Besides, we tell ourselves, the loss of privacy is inevitable.

Other times, we may add that we have nothing to hide. If you have nothing to hide, then you have no reason to worry about the proliferation of surveillance and tracking. Concerns about privacy are linked to suspicions of wrongdoing: only the people who are up to no good need to hide their tracks.

Ultimately, we may even suggest that there is something inauthentic or dishonest in wanting to safeguard our privacy. We should be the same in our private and in our public lives. Wanting to draw the curtains around our private lives suggests that we are somehow not truly our authentic selves while in the public eye. Again, what are you hiding?

Much of the discussion and scholarship around privacy place the individual and their rights at the centre of discussion. There is considerable debate about how we should conceptualize privacy: is it about controlling access to ourselves, the management of personal information, or specific rights like the right to control who can have my information and what they can do with it? What is the difference between privacy and solitude and how do we demarcate private spheres from public ones? Common themes include informed consent; control; contextual integrity; reasonable expectations; security; and integrity of our information.

This paper takes a different perspective to the matter of privacy in modern society. It shifts the perspective from asking how privacy is protected to asking what it protects and the interests that are at stake. I argue that privacy is important not because of privacy itself *per se*, but because privacy exists to protect, foster, and promote basic human dignity. This view of privacy changes how we think of our own individual privacy rights since privacy is about so much more than just my personal information. If privacy is, at its heart, about human dignity, then something is lost at a much more fundamental level when I dismiss my own privacy as irrelevant or unnecessary. Because I understand human dignity to be bound up in the fact that individuals are image-bearers of the Divine who are invested with moral autonomy, the diminishment of one individual's dignity is really an attack on the dignity of all humans. Thus, if privacy is about dignity, then the protection of my privacy is connected to my neighbor's dignity. I therefore shift the discussion of privacy from a question of individual rights to a broader set of issues. An analysis of the effect of digital technology on my personal privacy must become an analysis of how privacy violations affect human dignity and what duties I have to my neighbor as a result.

This analysis must also take into account the way that privacy rights are embedded in the social, political, and economic power structures of society. The protection of privacy is not extended in equitable ways in society. The ways that privacy is extended or withheld have material effects on the well-being and dignity of affected populations, but these populations generally have little agency in determining how their privacy will be mapped. Those with privilege have an obligation to be particularly mindful of how privacy protections are distributed in society. In the context of digital technology, we therefore have an obligation to critically assess how our own decisions to share our own personal information for our own convenience will affect the dignity of our neighbors. I will argue that digital technology does not exist for our convenience at all. Rather, it exists to consume our life experiences as raw materials used to create new types of assets in the big data economy that are subsequently used to further erode human dignity. As it is presently unfolding, the big data economy is toxic for individual dignity. As we wrestle with understanding how to think about privacy in the context of digital technology, we must keep the impact of big data on dignity at the forefront of our minds.

This paper will unfold as follows. Part II explores the concept of privacy and makes the case that privacy exists to protect human dignity. Part III places privacy in the context of embedded power dynamics in society and illustrates how extending or restricting privacy interests in different contexts can subvert dignity. In this part, I argue that privacy is not a leveler in society, and that, consequently, we must be particularly mindful of how patterns of privacy protection affect the well-being of vulnerable populations. Part IV analyzes how the big data economy affects privacy and dignity interests. I argue that big data and the emergence of surveillance capitalism exploit our willingness to share our life experiences in ways that fundamentally compromise human dignity. Part V concludes.

Part II: What does "privacy" mean?
Unpacking what "privacy" means is an essential starting point, though it is not an easy task. As a legal scholar, I am tempted to ground a discussion of privacy in its juridical context. Canadian and American privacy jurisprudence typically takes Warren and Brandeis's formulation of privacy as "the right to be left alone" as a starting point.[1]

In public law matters, privacy is connected to the constitutional right to protection against unreasonable search and seizure. In private law, the interest in privacy has traditionally engaged tort law and, to a certain extent, property law. Until relatively recently, courts were reluctant to recognize a free-standing right to privacy; instead, plaintiffs had to make their case using one of the more established torts, such as trespass to property, defamation, or nuisance. Dean Prosser's analysis of the case law[2] related to privacy, published in 1960, has been highly influential in shaping both Canadian and American courts' engagement with privacy in the tort law context. Prosser argued that case law supports four torts related to privacy: intrusion upon seclusion; public disclosure of embarrassing private facts; publicity that puts the plaintiff in a false light in the public eye; and appropriation of the plaintiff's name or likeness. Prosser's articulation of these four privacy torts was adopted by the *Restatement (Second) of Torts* (2010), and has been widely endorsed in Canadian and American jurisprudence.

There is another vast and important legal dimension to privacy: the law that governs when and how our personal data may be collected and used, especially for commercial purposes and surveillance. This dimension of privacy is bound up with questions about information: information about us (e.g., gender and age), information generated from us (e.g., tracking of our mobile phone's GPS), information shared by us (e.g., social media or information we disclose in confidence to, say, our doctor), and information about us gleaned from observation (e.g., surveillance cameras). As a general rule, law avoids a kind of protective paternalism that would simply prohibit the collection of our data, with or without consent. Instead, the law has focused on regulating access, control, and use of our personal information. Privacy law regimes establish requirements for obtaining "informed consent" and impose restrictions on how and when personal information can be shared with third parties. They seek to protect the integrity (that is, accuracy) of information and to ensure that people can access the information that has been collected about them. These regimes include requirements related to securing this information and providing remedies for unauthorized breaches, leaks, and uses.

A discussion of privacy law regimes engages questions about what the limits of privacy are. We wrestle with how to balance our individual rights to privacy with pressing social concerns about security and how to balance a privacy interest in non-disclosure with the right of another to freedom of expression. How much intrusive monitoring are we willing to accept to prevent a terror attack on domestic soil? If a person receives welfare, does the state have a fair interest in monitoring exactly how that person spends their welfare cheque? Should we use mass-collected data to develop algorithms that can then decide who should receive certain social benefits, which accused person should be released on bail, and how long a prison sentence should be? These types of questions force us to consider a more basic question: what are we trying to protect when we talk about privacy?

There is robust scholarly discussion about what privacy means, and this matter is not the domain of any particular one discipline. While there is considerable discussion of privacy[3], there is very little consensus on what privacy means or what it requires. In his review of the literature related to privacy, Lindsay observes that, "...the most notable feature of this [scholarship on privacy] has been an almost complete absence of agreement concerning both the definition of privacy and the values said to be promoted by the legal protection of privacy."[4] For his part, Solove captures the sprawling state of scholarship and the difficulties this breadth engenders as follows: "Privacy seems to be about everything, and therefore it appears to be nothing."[5]

If we are to have a meaningful discussion of privacy, we must make some choices, however arbitrary, about where to start. For the purposes of contributing to the exploration of the intersection of privacy, society, and faith, I will start by asking a lawyerly-type of question: what interest (or interests) are we protecting when we seek to safeguard privacy and what is at stake? This question transcends tort law, constitutional rights, and the regulation of access to information, and seeks insight into the values or interests that underpin these various areas of law.

When we excavate the law and policy of privacy, we find that a concern for basic human dignity lies close to the heart of privacy. My understanding of privacy in this regard is heavily influenced by Warren and Brandeis[6] and Bloustein[7], although given that privacy is linked to basic human dignity, the interest in protecting privacy has an ahistorical dimension. That is, the protection of privacy is not a modern phenomenon, nor does privacy exist as an artifact of western legal thought. The ways society has articulated the interest in privacy and the mechanisms adopted to protect it have evolved and shifted over time. For example, as I will discuss below, in ancient communities, where people lived cheek-to-jowl with each other, the sanctioning of gossip protected human dignity by effectively deeming some matters to be "off-limits" for public discussion. Moreover, an individual's inner thoughts, opinions, and preferences have always belonged to the individual alone, even when living in very close quarters. Certainly, modern technology has had a significant impact on how we understand and protect our interests in privacy. But the core nature of the interests at stake has always been directly related to basic human dignity and thus ahistorical in nature.

To understand the connection between human dignity and privacy, we must begin by recognizing its fundamental complexity: paradoxically, humans are individuals who are inherently social creatures in nature [what do you mean "in nature"? Humans in nature don't exist any longer]. I conceptualize humans to be created in the image of the Divine, a fact that bestows a special dignity on humans. Humans are moral agents, capable of making moral decisions and having individual agency in their lives (this is also a matter of belief only, so you must as well state it). At the same time, humans are also inherently social beings: as individuals, we find our truest expression in relation with each other. No need to repeat yourself, it is sufficiently clear already Thus, we are created as individuals yet we are also created for community.

Privacy mediates ourselves as individuals and ourselves as social beings and creates conditions for human flourishing. Needs rewriting. It exists as a duty that we owe to each other as image bearers of the Divine; this duty is also sometimes sanctioned by social norms and sometimes by legal principles. Privacy provides a sphere where individuals can become themselves, grow into their autonomy, and exercise their moral decision-making. What privacy actually means at any given time in terms of social norms and legal rights is a function of what human dignity requires in a particular historical context. Consequently, what we owed each other in terms of privacy one thousand years ago differs from what we owe each other today. Human dignity is the constant, not any particular iteration of the content of privacy.

Understood in this way, privacy has both a deontological and a teleological importance. We protect privacy both because of the duties we owe to each other and because of its central role in creating conditions where humans can thrive. Unpacking the deontological and teleological dimensions of privacy alongside of various ways that the interest in privacy has been articulated, will elucidate the close connection between human dignity and privacy.

From a deontological perspective, privacy exists as a duty we owe to others.[8] Affirming the dignity of each individual and honouring the God in whose image each individual has been made, begin by recognizing that each individual has inherent worth in and of their selves in and of themselves? Individuals should not be treated as a means to an end or as an object of public curiosity. We ought to regard each person as an individual with whom we can engage rather than as an object upon which we can act or a means that we can use to our own ends. Engaging with other individuals involves respecting boundaries set by those individuals and the choices they make, and not using the details of their lives to satiate our own curiosity or as fodder for gossip mills.

in the canon of Western philosophy Immanuel Kant provides one of the most important articulations of the nexus between human dignity and the duties we owe each other:

> [M]an, and in general every rational being, exists as an end in himself and not merely as a means to be arbitrarily used by this or that will. He must in all his actions, whether directed to himself or to other rational beings, always be regarded at the same time as an end .... Persons are, therefore, not merely subjective ends, whose existence as an effect of our actions has a value for us; but such beings are objective ends, ie, exist as ends in themselves.[9]

Kant argued that we have a duty to respect the inherent value and dignity of each individual and that this duty includes treating each person as an end in and of themselves. This Kantian imperative underlies a number of important accounts of the right to privacy, including that of Fried[10], Benn[11], and Reiman[12,13].

Some of the most familiar social norms related to privacy are tied to this duty to treat each person as an end in and of themselves. Take, for example, "peeping" or spying on someone. The uninvited gaze is offensive for a number of reasons, not the least of which is that it treats the observed person as an object and thus fails to show respect for that person. This is true even if the person being observed never becomes aware that they are being watched or recorded without their consent. Similarly, long-standing prohibitions on gossip, both in its casual form and its published form in tabloids, are connected to the way that gossip uses the details of personal, private lives as entertainment for third parties. As Hunt notes, "in each case, the wrongdoer is treating the victim as simply a *means* to an end (that is, to his own titillation, for the tom, and to boosting magazine sales, for the tabloid) rather than as *end in himself*. It is for this reason that many authors regard invasions of privacy as offences to dignity, in the Kantian sense.[14]

For scholars like Benn and Reiman, the duty we owe to each other to respect each other's privacy is directly connected to recognizing the personhood, and thus inherent dignity, of each other. For Benn, being a "person" means being one who is conscious of herself, who recognizes her own agency, and, crucially, who is a chooser.[15] How about if an individual is not aware of himself (unconscious, mentally challenged, senile, a baby?) Respecting others requires not just respecting their actual choices, but also their right to make a choice and their potential choices. Covert spying and other violations of privacy are egregious not just because a person has not given consent (made a choice) about the disclosure, but because these invasions treat the person's capacity to make a choice as irrelevant. In so doing, argues Benn, the intruder,

> fails to show a proper respect for persons; he is treating people as objects or specimens — like "dirt" — and not as subjects with sensibilities, ends, and aspirations of their own, morally responsible for their own decisions, and capable, as mere specimens are not, of reciprocal relations with the observer .... For this is to "take liberties", to act impudently, to show less than a proper regard for human dignity.[16]

Reiman argues that privacy is a complex set of social practice and behaviours that ultimately amount to a "*social ritual by means of which an individual's moral title to his existence is conferred.*"[17] Privacy is, for Reiman, a precondition to personhood, for to move from existing as a human being to a person, one must have a sense of self – a human who "regards his own existence – his thoughts, his body, his actions – as his *own.*"[18] Privacy, then, has a two-fold purpose with respect to personhood: first, it conveys to the developing child that she has exclusive moral rights over herself, and second, the social ritual of privacy confirms and conveys respect for the personhood of already-developed humans on an ongoing basis.[19]

Warren and Brandeis tie privacy (in their words, "the right to be left alone") to dignitary interests where the injury suffered is a lowering of a person's esteem of others. Violations of privacy injure a person's feelings, and this type of injury is as serious, if not more so, than any kind of physical harm.[20] When Warren and Brandeis talk about "injury to feelings", they refer to something more profound than merely a bruised ego. Indeed, Warren and Brandeis describe an invasion of privacy as a "spiritual injury" and suggest that what privacy protects is the right to "an inviolate personality".[21] Warren and Brandeis do not expand on the scope of this right. Blousein, however, interprets "inviolate personality" to mean "the individual's independence, dignity and integrity; it defines man's essence as a unique and self-determining being."[22] Building on the work of Warren and Brandeis, Bloustein argues that there is one central and fundamental interest that underpins the law related to privacy: human dignity. The privacy torts and statutory provisions that limit and protect mandatory disclosure of personal information,

> ...preserve dignity by restricting publicity, by assuring a man that his life is not the open and indiscriminate object of all eyes...by making a man secure in his person, not only against prying eyes and ears, but against the despair of being the subject of public scrutiny and knowledge.[23]

To be free from "prying eyes and ears" is no small thing. Yet, one of the most common arguments raised in response to concerns about privacy is, "I have nothing to hide and therefore I do not object to prying eyes and ears".[24] The "nothing to hide" argument is, according to Bruce Schneier, "the most common retort against privacy advocates".[25] In its simplest form, the "nothing to hide" argument is as follows, "if you are not doing anything wrong, then you have nothing to fear from surveillance, and if you are doing something wrong, then you do not have a legitimate interest in keeping your information private".

The "nothing to hide" argument has become especially prevalent in the post-9/11 world, where security concerns and "the war against terror" have been used to justify wide-spread collection of private communications and information. The post-9/11 context has allowed for the assertion of the argument in its most compelling form. Solove sets out the argument:

> The NSA surveillance, data mining, or other government information-gathering programs will result in the disclosure of particular pieces of information to a few government officials, or perhaps only to government computers. This very limited disclosure of the particular information involved is not likely to be threatening to the privacy of law-abiding citizens. Only those who are engaged in illegal activities have a reason to hide this information. Although there may be some cases in which the information might be sensitive or embarrassing to law-abiding citizens, the limited disclosure lessens the threat to privacy. Moreover, the security interest in

> detecting, investigating, and preventing terrorist attacks is very high and outweighs whatever minimal or moderate privacy interests law-abiding citizens may have in these particular pieces of information.[26]

As Solove goes on to argue, this version of the "nothing to hide" argument is formidable. It balances intrusions on an individual's privacy with national security concerns. Given the degree to which an individual's privacy is compromised and the counter-vailing interest in national security, it is not difficult to justify intrusions upon privacy.[27] However, as Solove argues, the "nothing to hide" argument, even in its strongest form, misses the point of privacy entirely. The core problem with this argument is that "it myopically views privacy as a form of concealment or secrecy."[28]

Viewing privacy in terms of protecting human dignity changes the calculus. We do not protect privacy to safeguard our secrets; we protect privacy because it is necessary for human dignity and for human flourishing. We protect privacy because we have a duty to uphold the inherent value and dignity of each individual by treating them as ends in and of themselves. We protect privacy because in so doing, we demonstrate respect for the basic personhood of others. We also protect privacy because humans seem to need places that are free from prying eyes and ears in order to become fully themselves. This brings us to a set of connections between privacy and human dignity that are more teleological in nature.[29]

Privacy serves the greater purpose (the *telos*) of human flourishing; for humans to thrive, they need space to develop their individual selves and to grow into becoming autonomous moral decision-makers. As I have pointed out earlier, individuals also need to cultivate relationships and to be part of community. Privacy plays a central role in creating conditions where humans can form meaningful relationships and share their lives in society without somehow also losing themselves in it.

Privacy allows a person to develop a sense of "self" in at least two important respects. First, it creates a space where an individual can become cognizant of his own self as separate from others. An individual can only be herself as a separate entity if there is a society, a collective, from which to withdraw and against which she may distinguish herself.

Our sense of having an individual self requires boundaries between ourselves and others; otherwise, we are simply absorbed into a faceless mass of humanity. As Simmel notes, individuals need to be able to retreat into a private sphere in order to develop as a "psychologically and socially distinct person."[30]

Second, privacy provides a realm where a person can develop her own views and preferences without the pressure to conform to social norms. Once a person is able to recognize herself as being separate from others, she is then able to begin to form her own set of preferences, thoughts, and opinions. As she does so, she moves toward becoming aware of her self as having moral autonomy. Her capacity to exercise meaningful morally autonomous decision-making will depend, as I discuss below, on a mix of important socio-cultural, political, and economic conditions. Indeed, I will argue that the contingency of an individual's full right to live and to act as a morally autonomous decision-maker is one of the reasons that privacy is so important and why we must have a broader sense of what is at stake when we make decisions about our own privacy.

The social pressure to conform and the human psyche itself create a need for privacy to mediate each person's individual self with the corresponding social self. There is an inherent tension in being both a social being and an individual with moral autonomy. As social beings, we need community; non-conformity with social norms and expectations risks our place in it. At the same time, full conformity would deaden those parts of us that make us unique individuals. Indeed, full conformity would make our individual moral autonomy moot since we would supplement our own reasoning and intuitions with whatever society tells us is right. which is the case in many societies of the past and now Privacy mediates the tension between our individuality and our need for community by creating a place of retreat, free from social scrutiny, where an individual can "be herself" without inhibition. Bloustein captures the importance of privacy in this regard as follows:

> [t]he man who is compelled to live every minute of his life among others and whose every need, thought, desire, fancy or gratification is subject to public scrutiny, has been deprived of his individuality and human dignity.... His opinions, being public, tend never to be

different; his aspirations, being known, tend always to be conventionally accepted ones; his feelings, being openly exhibited, tend to lose their quality of unique personal warmth and to become the feelings of every man. Such a being, although sentient, is fungible; he is not an individual.[31]

Psychologist Sidney Jourard provides an important account of why humans, as individuals who are also social beings, need a private sanctuary.[32] Jourard argues that as social beings, individuals live within different spheres of relationships and roles, each of which carries different responsibilities. Individuals feel pressure to ensure they meet society's expectations about their roles and to conform to behavioural norms associated with their roles. The pressure to conform and to meet obligations tends to constrain individuals, causing them to suppress thoughts, preferences, opinions, and actions that fall outside of accepted boundaries. This subversion of the individual's true self causes distress, anxiety, exhaustion, and even physical illness. In Jourard's view, individuals need a protected space where they can "simply *be* rather than *be respectable*."[33]

Reiman draws on Erving Goffman's study of "total institutions" to illustrate the effect of a total loss of privacy on the self.[34] Total institutions refer to institutions like prisons and asylums where inmates are completely cut off from the outside world and all dimensions of their lives are monitored and managed. Individual inmates are completely deprived of their privacy in these institutions. The effect of this complete deprivation is, to use Goffman's term, the mortification of the self: the invasion of privacy experienced by in-mates extends to all parts of themselves, with the ultimate effect of killing off the self, to use Reiman's words.[35] Reiman ultimately concludes that the social rituals of privacy are necessary and essential for individual to have moral ownership of herself.

Scholars differ on what privacy actually requires to provide an effective sanctuary for the self.[36] But there is little dispute that humans need a place where they are protected from prying eyes and ears for the sake of their general well-being. In *Campbell v. MGN Ltd.* (a leading UK case related to the tort of breach of confidence), Lord Nicholls captured the importance of privacy in this regard in his observation that "[a] proper degree of privacy is essential for the [well-being] and development of an individual"[37]

Scholars such as Fried[38], Benn[39], Rachels[40], Gavison[41], and Simmels[42] point to another way that privacy mediates the co-existences of our individual selves and our social selves: by making relationships possible. Fried makes the case forcefully: "...[privacy] is necessarily related to ends and relations of the most fundamental sort: respect, love, friendship and trust. Privacy is not merely a good technique for furthering these fundamental relations; rather without privacy they are simply inconceivable."[43] Fried recognized that meaningful relationships are forged when individuals share intimate actions, beliefs and emotions with each other; but if such intimacies were widely shared, they would cease to be intimacies altogether. For relationships to be deep and meaningful, there must be a degree of exclusivity in access.

Fried further argues that meaningful, intimate relations require the sharing of our selves with each other. But to share ourselves, we must develop a sense of self, and this requires privacy in the sense of being able to work through one's thoughts and consider whether to take a certain course of action or not before such thoughts and actions are revealed. If we were forced to reveal all our thoughts and musings, we would be deprived of the ability to choose whether to act on them. Moreover, we would almost certainly wound others if our intimate thoughts and opinions were revealed indiscriminately.[44]

Rachels makes a similarly forceful case that privacy is necessary to the formation and maintenance of relationships.[45] Rachels recognizes that our lives feature different roles and relationships, and we are therefore faced with shifting expectations and social norms. We adapt our behaviour according to the social context and the relationship in question; quite simply, we do not act the same way around our boss as we do around our best friend. Privacy gives us the flexibility and freedom to adapt our behaviour in response to the relational context and thus to maintain these relationships:

> We now have an explanation of the value of privacy in ordinary situations in which we have nothing to hide. The explanation is that, even in the most common and unremarkable circumstances, we regulate our behavior according to the kinds of relationships we

have with the people around us. If we cannot control who has access to us, sometimes including and sometimes excluding various people, then we cannot control the patterns of behavior we need to adopt (this is one reason why privacy is an aspect of liberty) or the kinds of relations with other people that we will have.[46]

Benn, Gavison, and Simmels also link privacy to the conditions necessary to form intimate relationships, including sexual and emotional relationships. Unfettered access to individuals makes it all but impossible to form meaningful relationships with a close, inner circle, much less be physically intimate with another. To exist as social beings means forming meaningful, intimate relationships; but one cannot have an intimate relationship with everyone. Intimacy implies limited access, and limited access ultimately means that the individual must have some privacy – freedom from access by everyone in order to give meaningful access to some.

In interpreting Article 17 of the International Covenant on Civil and Political Rights[47], the United Nations Human Rights Committee has stated that privacy includes the "sphere of a person's life in which he or she can freely express his or her identity, be it by entering into relationships with others or alone."[48] The European Court of Human Rights has also recognized that the protection of privacy guaranteed in Article 8 of the European Convention on Human Rights[49] is meant to create a protected sphere in which a person can develop, both as an individual and in relation to others. The Court stated that the protection under Article 8, "includes a person's physical and psychological integrity ... [and] is primarily intended to ensure the development, without outside interference, of the personality of each individual in his relations with other human beings".[50]

These articulations of the importance of privacy may initially seem incongruous with early human history. In ancient times, communities were so small and living quarters so intimate that a person would be hard-pressed to find spaces where they could be left alone, free from prying eyes and ears. It was all but impossible to keep others from knowing their business, at least insofar as their business meant day-to-day events and happenings. If humans really do need privacy as a basic condition for development and thriving, how have humans managed to survive thus far?

The answer, at least in part, is that what privacy requires to sustain human dignity shifts over time, alongside of cultural norms and practices. The needs of modern humans differ from those of early humans. Where once it was enough to have separate tents, we now need bricks and mortar to separate us (at least if you live in the West). Interestingly, the architecture of homes in the Middle East illustrates that protecting privacy has long been a central consideration in the day to day lives of people. In a literature review on the design of Muslim homes, Othman, Aird, and Buys find that the design of Muslim home "strictly follows the teachings from the Quarn, *sunnahs*, and *hadiths* to ensure that each home owner or dweller and his/her family are allowed to unwind and rest from the pressure and demands on the outside world."[51] From the outside world but not from each other! A Westerner would lose her mind in such a privacy, I know from experience, when a relative can enter your "private quarters any time!" Design took into account visual privacy, acoustic privacy, and even olfactory privacy.[52]

Islamic teachings prioritize safeguarding the privacy of the home. These teachings prohibit visual intrusion by looking into a neighbour's window.[53] The design of homes was therefore carefully structured to make it difficult for people to peer into someone else's home. For example, features such as the placement of doors and windows, the size of windows and doors, regulations about the height of buildings and balconies, and the use of internal courtyards and gendered spaces were used to safeguard visual privacy.[54] This is highly contestable. In a harem, for example, windows were tiny so that women could look outside without being seen.

Jewish law and teachings also place importance on personal privacy. Talmudic teachings protected privacy by restricting physical entry into people's homes. Rabbinic teachings prohibit the entry of one's neighbour's home without invitation; this prohibition extends even to the homes of family members and even in cases where a lender is seeking to procure the pledge that a debtor has promised to secure a debt.[55] However, in native Alaskan villages, for example, such a prohibition would be considered rude. People come in without invitation any time of the day or night.

Laws that prohibited uninvited looking (or visual prying) into the home complement the restrictions on physical entry into other people's homes. The Talmud teaches that when Balaam, an enemy prophet who was hired to curse the Israelites, looked out over the Jewish encampment, he spontaneously turned his curse into a blessing. According to Talmudic teaching, Balaam switched his curse to a blessing when he saw how the tents were aligned so that they did not face into each other, thus protecting each individual's privacy.[56] While this mutual respect for privacy began as a social virtue, during the "Mishnaic period the principle was formulated as a vested legal right that enabled a person to enjoin his neighbor against creating doors and windows in a manner that would injure his privacy."[57] Jewish building regulations, for example, contain rules about the construction of walls near a neighbour's window that were designed to protect both privacy (by preventing people from looking down or in) and light (by ensuring that the wall did not cast a shadow in the neighbour's home).[58] Regulations about the construction of parapets served the protection of privacy as well, in addition to safety-related concerns.[59]

Longstanding prohibitions against gossip and the significance of protecting information obtained in confidence are further illustrations of the ways that even ancient communities had regard for privacy. Jewish law (and Biblical teachings) prohibit "tale-bearing," which has been interpreted as disclosing confidential information[60] and as spreading gossip and slander[61], for example. We see, then, that while the boundaries of privacy may have been different in the past, boundaries existed all the same. The fact that privacy did not exist in its current form should not cause us to think that it did not exist at all.

There is one dimension of our human existence that has always been private: our own thoughts. Even when people live (or lived in) highly communal contexts, each individual's thoughts remained her own until she elected to share them. And the life of the mind is an important dimension of human life. One of the key attributes of being human is the ability to make autonomous moral decisions – to have opinions and preferences.[62] The inherent privacy of one's own thoughts illustrates the close connection between privacy and human dignity.

Privacy also enriches this most central element of being human by giving us space to develop, test, and refine our thoughts and viewpoints before sharing them more broadly.[63] Privacy, it is argued, is necessary for deep thinking, writing, and creating[64]; as Solove notes many of creators of great social, political, and artistic works began their work in solitude.[65] In this respect, privacy enables social flourishing, as well as individual flourishing, as individuals are able to share the work they have begun in private with a wider community.

In the Western tradition, privacy has been extended into the politico-legal realm in its service to the protection of human dignity. The expression of the right to individual moral decision-making has been interpreted as having the right to make decisions in matters that are of a purely private and personal nature; this right, in turn, is curiously bound up with the right to one's property. The Supreme Court of Canada provides a concise and helpful history in its decision in *R. v. Dyment*:

> ... The lives of people in earlier times centred around the home and the significant obstacles built by the law against governmental intrusions on property were clearly seen by Coke to be for its occupant's "defence" and "repose"; see *Semayne's Case* (1604), 5 Co. Rep. 91 a, 77 E.R. 194, at p. 91 b and p. 195 respectively. Though rationalized in terms of property in the great case of *Entick v. Carrington* (1765), 19 St. Tr. 1029, 2 Wils. K.B. 275, 95 E.R. 807, the effect of the common law right against unreasonable searches and seizures was the protection of individual privacy....[66]

Entick v. Carrington[67] established an important principle: the government can take no action against an individual unless specifically authorized by the law, but the individual has the right to do as he pleases unless the law specifically prohibits the act. This case provided the early foundations for the protection of privacy in so far as it established that agents of the state do not have unfettered right to pry into our personal lives, for example, through warrantless surveillance. *Entick v. Carrington* also set out an important connection between our private lives and our right to morally autonomous decision-making: when in the private realm, our personal choices are just that: personal and not subject to general regulation.[68]

As Lindsay notes, the Enlightenment political tradition was largely consumed with the question of defining the legitimate exercises of state power and the appropriate limits of this power.[69] Law played a central role in setting the boundaries for the legitimate exercise of political power: "an exercise of power was legitimate if it was in accordance with law."[70] Law, according to Lord Camden in *Entick v. Carrington*, existed to protect private property. Thus, property, political power, individual rights, and democratic rights began to converge, especially in the Lockean tradition.

Most of the serious considerations of the connection among privacy, the right to autonomy, and democracy in the Western tradition has come after Warren and Brandeis published their article asserting a "right to be left alone" in 1890. Since then, scholars have argued that privacy is necessary for the exercise of the freedom of expression[71], civic engagement and participation[72], the exercise of autonomy[73], and the very flourishing of democracy itself[74].

Part III: Privacy, dignity, and power

We cannot talk about privacy and dignity without also talking about power, for imbalances in power allow privacy to be withheld or sometimes imposed in ways that materially compromise human dignity. Take, for example, the case of enslaved people in the American south. Enslaved people worked constantly under the watchful (and often cruel) eye of over-seers. Their actions were monitored. Enslaved people were subject to a very different set of privacy norms than free people. Arguably, slavery could not have functioned without the excessive restrictions on the privacy of enslaved people. The justification for these restrictions were embedded in a perverse and inhumane denial of the very personhood and inherent dignity of enslaved people. The power that restricted the privacy of enslaved people was further emboldened by the de-humanization that flowed from these deprivations of privacy in the first place. In short, deprivation of privacy, denial of human dignity, and gross imbalances in power mutually re-enforced each other. This is as true today as it was in the American south at the time of slavery.

Privacy has also been imposed on people in ways that injure their basic dignity. In prisons, prisoners are sometimes disciplined or "managed" using solitary confinement, where the prisoner is restricted to a cell for 22-24 hour per day and is denied meaningful interactions with others.[75] A significant body of literature dating back to the 19th century demonstrates that prolonged solitary confinement commonly results in severe psychological and psychiatric harm.[76] Grassian describes the central features of the psychiatric syndrome that can result from solitary confinement as follows: "The paradigmatic psychiatric disturbance was an agitated confusional state which, in more severe cases, had the characteristics of a florid delirium, characterized by severe confusional, paranoid, and hallucinatory features, and also by intense agitation and random, impulsive, often self-directed violence."[77] Because of the significant psychological and psychiatric harms that flow from imposing total privacy, there are multiple international covenants, statements, and instruments that restrict or outright prohibit states from using their coercive power to hold detainees in solitary confinement for prolonged periods.[78]

The dichotomy between the public and the private realms has played a central role in diminishing the dignity of women, for example, by exposing them to the risk of domestic violence and by limiting their moral autonomy. Rebecca Green notes that feminists have long placed the public-private distinction at the centre of their critiques; historically, the public realm has been associated with political rights and economic activity, while most of "domestic" life was relegated to the private realm, where the state had limited authority to act.[79] According to Green, "[s]ince its inception, the [feminist] movement sought both to challenge the existence of the distinction itself and, short of that, at least to bring women more fully into the "public" realm.[80]

Feminists have understood how power becomes mapped onto claims about privacy (both in granting privacy and in restricting it) in ways that threaten the basic safety and well-being of women in abusive relationships. In the Anglo-American tradition, early laws in England and America protected a husband's right of "chastisement" of their wives, that is, the right of husbands to use corporeal punishment on their wives.[81] The relationship between a husband and a wife was, in the eyes of the law, a private matter and thus not subject to the scrutiny of the state. This approach to privacy ensured that a wife would not enjoy the protection of the state against violence committed against her by her spouse. Later laws and judicial pronouncements focused explicitly on the "evolving right of privacy" and the need to protect people from public embarrassment. Green cites the example of an 1868 judicial decision in which the court held, "[H]owever great are the evils of ill temper, quarrels, and even personal conflicts inflicting only temporary pain, they are not comparable with the evils which would result from raising the curtain, and exposing to public curiosity and criticism, the nursery and the bed chamber."[82]

Laws have changed, and domestic violence has been criminalized. Claims to privacy, whether in terms of a protected sphere of action outside the public realm or a right to be protected against prying eyes and ears, no longer shield perpetrators of violence. Yet, claims related to privacy continue to imperil victims of domestic abuse. Now, however, the claims are not about shielding actions, but rather about having access to legal and court documents that contain sensitive information about a victim of abuse. Courts are public institutions and their records are, by and large, public, although courts retain a right to issue non-publication bans and to seal documents and records. The over-riding presumption, however, is that of openness. Given that many courts now publish records online, the openness of courts creates a very real risk that perpetrators of violence can use court records to track their victims down and hurt them.[83]

In the context of domestic violence, privacy typically does not serve to protect the basic safety, much less dignity, of the victims. Instead, privacy has been aligned with the interests of the more powerful abuser: first, by asserting the abuser's own privacy to shield the acts of violence from outside scrutiny, and then by denying the victim's right to privacy in court records that contain sensitive information. Privacy has not developed in ways that robustly protect the vulnerable in abusive relationships; on the contrary, it has been weaponized in ways that allow the perpetuation of abuse.

The lesson here is that privacy does not operate in a vacuum. Privacy is inherently a social matter: we would not need privacy if we lived in total solitude. Because privacy exists in the context of social relationships, it also exists within the political, social, and economic power dynamics of those relationships. Privacy is *not* a leveler of power; on the contrary, it can be given and withheld in ways that replicate and re-enforce existing power imbalances. To the extent that power imbalances prejudice the more vulnerable party's dignity (and they typically do), privacy (whether extending it or withholding it) can be co-opted in ways that subvert rather protect human dignity. Consequently, if we are truly concerned about our neighbour's welfare, then we must think critically about what human dignity requires in a particular context and, from there, determine how privacy should be articulated in that context. In the next, and final, section, I will outline some of the considerations relevant to privacy that arise when we ask ourselves what human dignity may require in our current hyper-technological society.

Part IV: What dignity requires: considerations about privacy and digital technology

Social upheaval typically accompanies advances in technology: the invention of the printing press, the steam engine, mechanized forms of mass production, the modern computer, the internet, the personal computer, and digital technology have all brought major social change. Arguably, digital technology has led to the greatest upheaval in the shortest amount of time. Digital technology is more of a process than a thing, per se. Broadly put, digital technology refers to the way that information is captured, reduced to packets of data, transferred, and re-assembled in meaningful ways. "Information" in this context includes visual and auditory information; digital technology is the backbone of our modern communications system.

Digital technology is pervasive in industrialized countries. It underpins communications, banking, transportation, and virtually every other important public utility. It has changed how and where we shop, the nature of work, and the rudimentary elements of our day-to-day lives. Our home appliances are increasingly digitized in ways that allow data to be collected and exchanged with central sources through the internet. Digital technology also underlies a wide range of new appliances and devices, such as home assistants, home monitoring tools, and "smart" phones and "smart" watches. We are told that these devices and technologies improve our lives by giving us convenient "solutions" to things, like the ability to order groceries online or to turn the heat on at home before we arrive at the end of the day. We are told that these technologies make us safer and that they can help us improve our economic position by giving us opportunities to earn money through "side gigs" like driving for Uber. We are told that digital technology can make government processes more efficient. Digital technologies, we are promised, make services more accurate and our own experiences in a range of activities, from going to the doctor to shopping for new shoes to listening to music more "customized" and thus more "optimized."

What we often do not realize is that digital technology requires a critical input to generate much of its promised benefits: information. The value digital technology provides is bound up in its ability to collect, transmit, store, and sort vast amounts of data; the "raw product," so to speak, for digital technology is information about everyone and everything. As it turns out, digital technology itself has provided highly effective means for monitoring and for hoovering up information about the "who, where, what, and how" of our day-to-day lives.[84] Tech giants like Facebook, Alphabet (which owns Google), Twitter, and Amazon have also been highly adept at convincing people to share their personal information; in many cases, all it takes is offering free access to the platform's services.

In the past, we conveyed information about ourselves and others in person, by mail, and, in more recent times, telegram and telephone. The modes of communication constrained the diffusion of information. For example, a letter-carrier would not have any way of knowing what a letter said unless the letter was opened, and the law strictly prohibited this type of intervention. Surveillance required a concerted effort to intercept mail and phone calls. By contrast, the technology we use to communicate today is not blind to the content and location of our exchanges. On the contrary, the technology not only transmits the message, but it assembles a record of the message, including data about its contents, when it was sent, the identity of the sender and recipients, the location of the parties, and so on. This information is aggregated and analyzed; it is used to generate targeted advertising; it is exchanged, sold, and cross-referenced with other collections of data. In short, access to platforms like Facebook is not free; we trade access to our personal information for access to the platforms.

Digital technology has given rise to "big data." "Big data" refers to the vast quantities of data that are being captured by actors such as businesses, institutions, and governments on a daily basis. This data may be structured (that is sorted and organized) or unstructured. The data is generated from a wide range of sources, including mobile phone use, internet searches, sensors on shipping containers and cars, smart watches, and home monitoring systems, to name just a few. Collections of data have grown exponentially as technology allows for new ways of collecting information, new ways of tracking information, new types of information to collect, and new ways of understanding and processing this information.[85]

As the amount of available data expands exponentially and as methods improve to extract value from this data, big data has become a very valuable asset. Our personal information is so valuable in the modern, tech-based economy that it has been described as the "new gold" or the "new oil."[86] In 2012, the World Economic Forum issued a report[87] and a call-to-action that identified the potential value of big data as a tool for identifying needs, providing services, and predicting and preventing crises; the report urged political leaders and policy makers to become catalysts in the new "data ecosystem" by opening up their own datasets. The report also noted that in order to develop this data ecosystem, "business models must be created to provide the appropriate incentives for private-sector actors to share and use data for the benefit of society."[88]

Digital technology and big data clearly have significant implications for privacy. Scholars like Zuboff[89], Myers West[90], and Yeung[91] make compelling arguments about the central role that surveillance, mass predictive personalization, and the sale of personal data have in the modern economy. These scholars draw attention to the troubling way that the market seeks to leverage big data. Big data does not just gather vast amounts of personal data; big data analyzes the personal information of a large number of people across a population to discern trends and patterns using machine learning. This analysis yields behavioural data about an individual's likely preferences, interests, and traits; this data is then used to create what Zuboff calls "prediction products": calculations that anticipate what we will do next.[92] The results are highly detailed user profiles containing predictions about the users' future choices and actions. These profiles are traded among data brokers and purchased by advertisers yielding annual revenues in the hundreds of billions of dollars.[93] The opaque nature of the generation and trade of these profiles makes it very difficult for users to appreciate what happens to their data.[94]

What happens next makes trends in the big data economy especially pernicious: the behavioural predictions are used to nudge users toward certain actions. The response of users to these behavioural nudges is also recorded, analyzed, and then used to make the prediction model better; these feedback loops are powered by ever-stronger forms of computing such that the loops are updating and operating continuously.[95] The goal is simple: develop near-perfect prediction of user activity in real time, aided significantly by processes that nudge the user to act in certain ways. In other words, tech companies like Google and Facebook use people's data to sell prediction products while at the same time using this data to push people toward acting in ways consistent with their own prediction products (and their own profitability).[96]

The operation of markets in user data and the surveillance economy as a whole clearly raise significant concerns about the protection of privacy. From a dignity-centred approach, there are at least three material issues that must be addressed as society grapples with how to think about privacy in an era of big data, namely, the objectification of the self; authentic autonomy and consent; and presumptive data processing.

The objectification of the self

In the big data economy, human experience serves as the raw materials for the creation of value. To be clear, it is not just personal information, such as one's name and favourite sports team, that is collected. Big data captures as much of the dynamics of our everyday lives as it can: where we live; how well we sleep and how much we sleep; where we shop; when we shop; how fast we drive, walk, or run; our resting heart rate; how long we spend on any particular webpage; our browsing history; milestone events in our lives; relationships; our physical health; who we message and about what; the different ways we communicate to different people; our physical health; and our financial health: quite simply, everything. We are observed, constantly. What's more, while we exchange some of our data for free access to platforms like Twitter or Facebook, we also purchase devices like fitness trackers and apps like online nutrition diaries that also harvest our data.

"Smart home" assistants like Siri and Alexa are excellent examples of how we have invited (and paid) Big Data to enter our homes. Under the guise of offering us convenience, companies like Google, Amazon, and Apple have found a way to convince us to open our homes to continuous monitoring and data collection. Smart home assistants typically work by responding to a voice prompt (often called a "wake word") like "hey

Alexa...". This means that Alexa must remain on and listening even when you are not engaging with the device so that it will be ready to respond to a prompt. While it may be possible to disable the wake word systems, the default settings are always set to "on".

The growing use of facial recognition and other biometric information extends the reach of big data to even more intimate elements of our lives. The AI Now Institute reports that governments and companies are rolling out the use of facial recognition in contexts such as public housing, hiring, city streets.[97] China has aggressively rolled out facial recognition technology, using it for surveillance (including monitoring of school children in classrooms), to pay for services like public transit, to augment human identity checks, and even as a pre-condition to obtaining services like mobile telephony.[98]

The widespread harvesting and use of the human experience treat humans as objects – as things to be observed, monitored, and surveilled rather than as individual humans with which to engage. This objectification diminishes the basic dignity of humans as image-bearers of the Divine. Instead of honouring the Divine's image, big data attempts to commodify it.

The pervasive monitoring and collection of personal data also give us less and less space to be free from prying eyes and ears. Indeed, "smart" home devices and assistants have ensured that even the places where we should feel most secure and at ease – our homes – do not provide a refuge from surveillance. Big data has, however, provided us with a range of technology that it promises can enhance the security of our homes. An excellent example is Amazon's Ring service. Ring is a "smart" doorbell that features a camera with remote access and two-way audio. This enables a user to see outside their home even if they are away, as well as to communicate with visitors outside their doors remotely. Amazon also offers an app service called Neighbors by Ring, which allows users to view video uploaded to the app by other ring owners.

In August 2019, *The Guardian* reported that Ring has formed extensive partnerships with hundreds of US law enforcement agencies.[99] Pursuant to these partnerships, Ring provides police departments with free access to its platform (i.e., to video footage uploaded by Ring users) in exchange for outreach with local residents. According to *The Guardian*, these partnerships allow Ring to "to shape the communications of police departments it collaborates with, directing the departments' press releases, social media posts and comments on public posts."[100] Critics argue that these for-profit partnerships enable police to engage citizens in a way that allows police to obtain far more surveillance video than would be possible using a traditional warrant.[101]

Other apps such as NextDoor allow community members to share information about what they deem is "suspicious behaviour," while *Quartz* describes Citizen (another neighbourhood security app) as "a police scanner on steroids" which "brings the practice of eavesdropping on police scanners...into the mainstream, making it easy and digestible for everyone".[102] According to their proponents, these apps allow people to participate in a type of digital neighbourhood watch – with the added "benefit" that that personal interactions are not necessary.[103]

The deployment of Ring technology and apps such as NextDoor and Citizen enable private citizens to participate in the monitoring and surveillance of other citizens – but only if they are affluent enough to afford the enabling technology and have the time to spend on the apps. In other words, time and money allow some people to participate in the objectification of individuals through surveillance. In the case of NextDoor, this surveillance was further tainted by racial profiling; in 2015, journalist Sam Levin broke the story that NextDoor users "frequently post unsubstantiated "suspicious activity" warnings that result in calls to the police on Black citizens who have done nothing wrong."[104] Being a person of colour made it more likely that an individual would be reduced to an object of suspicion, deepening the marginalization already experienced by these individuals.

It seems that tech companies have managed to convince individuals to compromise the privacy and security of their own homes by bringing in smart home assistants while also convincing people that their security can be bolstered by surveilling their neighbours. Thus, not only are tech companies reducing their users to objects but they are also finding ways to nudge their users into objectifying other individuals – and all the while making a tidy profit. This profit surely comes at the cost of human dignity.

As the earlier discussion about privacy and dignity indicated, maintaining zones of privacy where we are able to limit access in various degrees to ourselves is essential to the development of our selves as morally autonomous agents, to the creation of meaningful relationships, and to general human flourishing. In the big data economy, we have allowed large swaths of the human experience to be observed, measured, analyzed, and commodified; in an important sense, big data has co-opted us in the mortification of our own selves. It is too soon to understand what the consequences of this mortification are for human dignity and human flourishing. But Westin's words, published in 1967, ring ominously today: "[N]o individual can play indefinitely, without relief, the variety of roles that life demands.... Privacy in this aspect gives individuals, from factory workers to Presidents, a chance to lay their masks aside for rest. To be always 'on' would destroy the human organism."[105]

Authentic autonomy and consent

The relationship between autonomy and big data is complex. While humans are individually autonomous decision-makers, we also exist in community together. Our moral autonomy exists in a relational context, and our behaviours are governed not just by our own preferences, but by laws, market forces, and social norms. In the context of a highly connected, data-driven society, individuals can leverage digital technology in its various forms to construct their own selves, including the social dimension of their selves. Bannerman explains:

> ... First, we use networks, technologies, techniques, and services to construct ourselves: to self-monitor and govern our health, physical activity, sleep, diets, and our own thinking and learning processes. Second, we form the self in relation with others, through networks of relations.[106]

Virtual communities offer opportunities for the creation of shared meanings and the enhancement of elements of the self that are paralleled in other individuals located in geographically distant places. Individuals are able to explore dimensions of themselves online that would be impossible to do in their physical location, including the exploration of taboo interests. Access to significant amounts of information about oneself, others, and the world at large offer resources that could be used in the process of developing one's own sense of self and in exercising moral autonomy. Digital technology, information communications infrastructure, and big data seem to offer resources that could enhance autonomy and thus enrich human dignity.

Implicit in this argument is the assumption that an individual can make meaningful choices about sharing her personal information: that she knows what information is collected, how it will be used, and who will use it. It also assumes that an individual can make meaningful choices about the information she is receiving. Before she makes a decision based on what her fitness tracker is telling her, for example, she must be able to trust that the data she is given is authentic (actually generated from her use of the tracker), accurately measured, and accurately displayed.

If she makes a decision about where to eat dinner based on a Google search of "good food nearby," her choice is only fully autonomous if Google has shown her all the options, not just the places that have paid for higher rankings on Google searches and not just the places that other people in the area seem to have preferred. The problem then becomes one of efficiency: the individual wants to make a decision without having to wade through dozens of reviews and websites. It is convenient to have Google to have sift through all the information for her and then present her with a curated list. She likely does not know why Google gave her this particular list, and she may not care. But the truth is that the list she is given, and upon which she will make a decision, is created using predictive algorithms fed by big data. When she ultimately makes her decision, it is likely that her phone will track her location; if she uses her credit card, there will be a record of where she ate and how much she spent. This and other information generated from this experience will be then become part of the feedback loop that will be used to shape her decision the next time she needs to decide where to eat. Given the role that nudging and predictive algorithms play in her decision-making process, how much autonomy has she meaningfully exercised?

As this example suggests, convenience in the big data economy typically requires that we compromise our ability to make autonomous decisions in return for efficient access to information. This might be justifiable if we had a good sense of what we are exchanging and how information is curated for us; in this case, we would be able to make a meaningful choice because we would have an understanding about how our own autonomy would be constrained in the decision-making process.

The power dynamics in the big data ecosystem, however, ensure that while ample data of individuals is available for collection, very little information about how this data is actually used is disclosed by the tech companies.

Tech companies leverage their power (economic, social, and political) to maintain information asymmetries. While the companies know a great deal about their users, their users and the general public know very little about the algorithms that are used in big data processes. Tech companies are notoriously un-transparent, using a variety of tactics, from selling information through data brokers to asserting intellectual property rights over algorithms, to render their data usage processes opaque.[107] As concerns *their* information, tech companies assert a right to total privacy. But where individuals' privacy is concerned, tech companies offer empty platitudes and promises. Their business models are predicated on harvesting personal data in the private spheres of life, after all.

Tech companies justify their intrusions on individual privacy by arguing that users consent to the collection and use of their information. User agreements typically include reference to a company's privacy policy, and by law, companies must have a privacy policy in place in a wide range of jurisdictions. However, tech companies tend to make these policies cumbersome, long, and difficult to understand. A study conducted in 2008 found that the average length of the privacy policies of American companies was 2500 words and would take ten minutes to read.[108] Moreover, a 2018 study confirmed what most people already know: the vast majority of people do not read the Terms of Service or the privacy policies of social networking services.[109] In fact, a Pew Research Center study from 2014 found that half of Americans do not know what a privacy policy is.[110] In this context, it seems disingenuous for tech companies to suggest that their users really do consent to all the ways that their personal information is collected, used, and shared.

The power of tech companies to offer their services on a "take it or leave it" basis and their sheer economic and political clout allow these companies to maintain significant asymmetries in privacy.[111] Their practices demonstrate a lack of regard for their users as autonomous individuals capable of (and entitled to) make moral decisions for themselves. Their disregard for the autonomy of their users is not surprising, however, given that they are not in the business of serving their users; they are in the business of harvesting and monetizing the everyday experiences of their users.

The fact that most people seem resigned to the fact that they have little control over the collection and the use of their data should not be misinterpreted as implying that people have made peace with the loss important elements of their autonomy. On the contrary, a 2019 Pew Research Center report, many Americans are concerned about the extent of data collection and the security of their information. This report made several significant findings.[112] First, Americans understand that their online activities are being tracked and, significantly, more than 60% of people "believe it is not possible to go through daily life without having their data collected by companies (62%) or the government (63%)."[113]

Second, most Americans believe that the risks posed by the collection of their personal data outweighs the benefits to them: "About eight-in-ten (81%) Americans say the potential risks outweigh the benefits when it comes to companies collecting data. When government collection of data is considered, 66% of adults agree."[114] Yet very few Americans believe that they understand what is being done with the information about them, and while the vast majority of people have been asked to consent to privacy policies, most do not bother to read the terms (either at all or in detail).[115] Finally, "[m]ore than eight-in-ten (84%) of Americans say they feel very little or no control over the data collected about them by the government, and 81% say the same when company data collection is considered."[116]

This Pew Research Center report suggests that many Americans no longer have a sense of agency when it comes to the monitoring of their day to day lives: their data will be collected and used in ways that they do not fully understand and in ways that are more likely to expose them to harm than good. Big data practices and the surveillance economy have disenfranchised people of their own sense of autonomy.

Presumptive data processing

One of the most pernicious effects of the use of big data on dignity is what I will call "presumptive data processing" ("PDP"). PDP refers to the creation and deployment of what Zuboff calls "prediction profiles" and the "behavioural surplus".[117] PDP is premised on the idea that it is possible to know an individual based on aggregated information about that individual. In this regard, PDP relies on artificial social cognition, that is, using data processing systems to attribute mental states to an individual based on the assumption that the individual will have aims, preferences, and motivations that are like people who are superficially similar to the individual.[118]

PDP, then, is about presumptions: presuming to know how people think and act; presuming that it is possible to categorize people in ways that will reliably predict their next move; and presuming that an individual is nothing more than the sum of the data she has left behind. PDP attempts to reduce individuals to algorithmic results and then, equally audaciously, nudge those individuals toward acting in a manner consistent with those results by controlling the information that is available to them.[119]

PDP fundamentally undermines human dignity. As King notes, "To deal with a person by treating her as a member of a group is not to deal with her as an individual person per se. Rather, it is to deal with her more like an object among other objects."[120] Moreover, the presumptiveness that underpins PDP limits human autonomy and does so with a view to monetizing the control of human choice. PDP is not just about predicting what an individual will do based on the individual's superficial resemblance with others; PDP seeks to direct human action. Zuboff argues that surveillance capitalism, "produces the possibility of modifying the behaviors of persons and things for profit and control."[121] Thus, PDP deals another, significant blow to dignity by seeking to constrict the opportunities for individual self-formation and discovery.

Privacy affords an individual the opportunity to become her own self, free from the types of prying ears and eyes that might otherwise pressure the individual to conform to society's expectations and norms. Surveillance capitalism goes beyond obliterating this type of privacy; it makes the concept of conformity moot. Conformity implies a measure of choice. PDP and surveillance capitalize maintain the illusion of choice while actively subverting meaningful autonomy by manipulating the information available to each individual within their own technological network:

> Conformity is no longer a 20th century-style act of submission to the mass or group, no loss of self to the collective produced by fear or compulsion, no psychological craving for acceptance and

belonging. Conformity now disappears into the mechanical order of things and bodies, not as action but as result, not cause but effect. Each one of us may follow a distinct path, but that path is already shaped by the financial and, or, ideological interests that imbue Big Other and invade every aspect of "one's own" life.[122]

Technology threatens to supplant the role that privacy now plays in mediating the co-existence of our individual selves and our social selves. Ironically, technology increasingly makes it possible for us to side-step navigating the social norms and legal rules about privacy by reducing the need and opportunity for interaction with other individuals. Consider, for example, the fact that supermarkets are replacing cashiers with automatic check-outs; online shopping has done considerable damage to the existence of traditional "brick and mortar" retail settings; and advanced communications infrastructure and cloud competing now obviate the need for offices in many cases. Technology, including PDP, diminishes human dignity by reducing the significance of human interactions in our lives, thus essentially all but eliminating the need for and the vestiges of privacy:

> As artificial systems become increasingly involved in our lives and assume roles that other humans have, our relationships built around reactive attitudes may be displaced by relationships dominated by the statistical stance and presumptuous aim attributions. If so, then we should worry that, in being increasingly treated as mere objects, we increasingly come to be mere objects.[123]

A key feature of PDP is mass personalization, which refers to the way that the predictions and nudges generated by big data are scaled up, but are also highly personalized to specific individuals.[124] PDP sorts and categorizes individuals and then, based on inferences obtained in this process, pushes out specific content to specific individuals. As a result, individuals are nudged in different ways, using different content, and hence the way that PDP affects their autonomy differs, too.

The algorithms used in PDP to facilitate mass personalization are well-known to be biased.[125] Algorithms prefer individuals who already enjoy a degree of privilege in society. They tend to replicate existing patterns of power in terms of the options presented to users, which ultimately has the effect of amplifying these patterns. For example, a 2015

Carnegie Mellon research study found that male users were shown six times more high paying job ads than their female counterparts.[126] In the fall of 2019, Apple and Goldman Sachs faced allegations of gender bias after a user was extended a significantly higher line of credit compared to his wife, whose official credit score is better than that of the user. Around the same time, the news broke that the "risk prediction" algorithm used by a major provider of healthcare in the United States generated racially-biased results, resulting in less care being extended to black patients. Amazon piloted software to automate its hiring process in 2014, but abandoned the project a few years later because women were being systematically excluded from job searches.

In short, the biases embedded in the algorithms used in PDP result in less opportunities being extended to women, people of colour, and other vulnerable groups. PDP undermines human dignity in this context by excluding certain people from the group of individuals who receive information about opportunities related to important things like employment, credit, housing, and education. Because the biases at play are generally based on personal traits that are difficult or impossible to change, PDP risks creating entrenched patterns of bias in mass personalization.

Moreover, the opacity of PDP tends to mask the problem, making it practically impossible for individuals to know the extent to which the opportunities offered to them differ from those offered to others, much less how and why a PDP system determines what will be offered to them at all.[127] This lack of explanation and accountability take their own toll on human dignity. La Fors, Custers and Keymolen observe,

> [b]eing confronted with discriminating profiles and opaque data-driven decisions, a citizen may experience a Kafkaesque situation in which her view and agency no longer is acknowledged. When a person no longer is treated as someone with particular interests, feelings and commitments, but merely as a bundle of data, her dignity may be compromised.[128]

Privacy is rarely extended in equal measure to everyone. PDP compounds the harm done to human dignity by replicating existing systems of power and oppression in its interference with the autonomy of individuals. It then deepens the harm by obfuscating the reasons for the prediction profiles it assigns each individual. Individuals are left in personalized boxes without knowing how big or how small their box is; sometimes, perhaps, even many times, individuals may not realize that they are in a box at all. In this respect, the violations of privacy occasioned by big data and surveillance capitalism are particularly insidious. Violations of privacy in the past were easier to detect. Digital technology allows for pervasive, stealthy infringements on privacy that steadily erode our basic dignity in almost imperceptible ways. In this context, we have a weighty responsibility to stay alert to the how digital technology shifts the landscape of human dignity, especially because the most vulnerable individuals in society are disproportionately affected by these shifts but less able to respond effectively.

Conclusion

At first glance, privacy may appear to be a quaint but antiquated idea. Digital technology has transformed society such that we now expect to be monitored in various aspects of our lives. We also accept and even embrace the extensive proliferation of technical devices in all corners of our lives. Indeed, we likely rely on those devices, along with modern communication networks, to make a range of decisions each day. Modern technology affords us many luxuries, and tech companies rely on our addiction to their services to safeguard their interest in hoovering up as much detail as possible about our day to day lives.

The question that we must ask, loudly and often, is: at what cost? The battle in the big data ecosystem is not over privacy rights; it is about basic human dignity. In the big data ecosystem, humans are not image-bearers of the Divine; we are merely bundles of data waiting to be monetized. Indeed, even our autonomy is another asset to be captured, managed, and monetized.

Honouring the Divine in whose image we are created and caring for our neighbour demand a response. There are no easy answers. We must start by asserting that nothing is inevitable and then we must work to be more conscious and conscientious consumers of digital technology. The first step is reframing questions about privacy in the big data ecosystem as questions about dignity. We must then evaluate digital technology using dignity as the primary lens of analysis, with a special view to the effects of technology on vulnerable populations. One of our central tasks is learning what questions to ask and then demanding responses from tech companies. We must insist on accountability.

Protecting human dignity in the big data ecosystem actually requires us to step into those aspects of ourselves that are uniquely human and thus intimately bound up with our dignity: our capacity for autonomous, moral reasoning. To safeguard our autonomy in the future, we must actively assert our autonomy now. The risk is real: we must literally use it or lose it.

Notes

1. See Samuel Warren & Louis Brandeis, "The Right to Privacy" (1890) 4 Harv. L. Rev. 193.
2. William Prosser, Privacy, (1960) 48 Cal. L. Rev. 383.
3. For good overviews of the field, see e.g., Daniel J. Solove, "A Taxonomy of Privacy" (2006) 154 U Pa L Rev 477 (Solove, "Taxonomy"); Daniel J. Solove, A Brief History of Information Privacy Law in PROSKAUER ON PRIVACY, PLI (2006) (Solove, "History"); Chris DL Hunt, "Conceptualizing Privacy and Elucidating its Importance: Foundational Considerations for the Development of Canada's Fledgling Privacy Tort" (2011) 37:1 Queens LJ 167; David Lindsay, "An Exploration of the Conceptual Basis of Privacy and the Implications for the Future of Australian Privacy Law" (2005) 29:1 Mel UL Rev 131; and Ryan, Michael, Persona Non Data: How Courts in the EU, UK and Canada are Addressing the Issue of Communications Data Surveillance vs. Privacy Rights (July 26, 2016). TPRC 44: The 44th Research Conference on Communication, Information and Internet Policy 2016. Available at SSRN: https://ssrn.com/abstract=2742157 or http://dx.doi.org/10.2139/ssrn.2742057.
4. Lindsay, *ibid.* at 135.
5. Daniel J. Solove, "Taxonomy", *supra* note 3 at 479.
6. Warren & Brandeis, *supra* note 1.
7. Edward J. Bloustein, "Privacy as an Aspect of Human Dignity: An Answer to Dean Prosser" (1964) 39 N Y U L Rev 962.
8. Given that the duties we owe to each other flow from the commandments we receive from God, these duties are also owed in a fundamental way to God.
9. Imanuel Kant, *Grounding for the Metaphysics of Morals; with On a Supposed Right to Lie Because of Philanthropic Concerns* (trans J Ellington) 3rd ed (Indianapolis: Hackett Publishing Company, 1993) at 428.
10. Charles Fried, *Privacy* (1968) 77 Yale Law Journal 475 ("Privacy"). See also Charles Fried, *An Anatomy of Values: Problems of Personal and Social Choice* (Boston: Harvard University Press, 1970).
11. Stanley Benn, 'Privacy, Freedom, and Respect for Persons' in J Roland Pennock & John Chapman (eds), *Nomos XIII: Privacy* (New York: Atherton Press, 1971) 1.
12. Jeffrey Reiman, "Privacy, Intimacy, and Personhood" (1976) 6:1 Phil & Pub. Aff. 26.
13. Fried, Benn, and Reiman are among the most prominent scholars who take a Kantian approach to privacy, but they are not the only ones. For good overviews of the accounts of Kantian and deontological approaches to the right to privacy, see Lindsay, *supra* note 3,

Hunt, *supra* note 3, and N.A. Moreham, "Why is Privacy Important? Privacy, Dignity, and Development of the New Zealand Breach of Privacy Tort" in Jeremy Finn & Stephen Todd, eds., *Law, Liberty, Legislation* (LexisNexis New Zealand, 2008) 231-248.

14. Hunt, *supra* note 3 at 204, citations omitted, emphasis in original.
15. Benn, *supra* note 11 at 8–9.
16. *Ibid.*
17. Reiman, *supra* note 12 at 39, emphasis in original.
18. *Ibid*, emphasis in original.
19. *Ibid.*
20. Warren & Brandeis, *supra* note 1 at 197.
21. *Ibid.* at 205.
22. Bloustein, *supra* note 7 at 971.
23. *Ibid.* at 1000.
24. For an excellent and detailed analysis of the "nothing to hide" argument, see Daniel J. Solove, "'I've Got Nothing to Hide' and Other Misunderstandings of Privacy" (2007) 44 San Diego L Rev 745 ("Nothing").
25. Bruce Schneier, Commentary, *The Eternal Value of Privacy*, WIRED, May 18, 2006, http://www.wired.com/news/columns/1,70886-0.html. See also Geoffrey R. Stone, Commentary, *Freedom and Public Responsibility*, CHI. TRIB., May 21, 2006, who calls the argument "an all-too-common refrain" (at 11).
26. Solove, "Nothing", *supra* note 24 at 753.
27. *Ibid.*
28. *Ibid.* at 765. In his article, Solove articulates his own theory of privacy, which views privacy as having several, related facets that protect different interests in different contexts. Solove has developed a taxonomy of privacy in an attempt to identify and elucidate these various facets of privacy. Solove summarizes his taxonomy in his paper on the "Nothing to Hide Argument"; the taxonomy itself is laid out in detail in his article entitled "A Taxonomy of Privacy" (*supra* note 3).
29. One of the most common forms of teleological arguments is utilitarianism, a framework that justifies outcomes on the grounds of maximizing overall welfare. Utilitarianism is commonly expressed as the principle that we ought to prefer options that provide the greatest good for the greatest number. However, my next set of arguments are not strictly utilitarian in nature. Instead, they focus on the ways that privacy serves the overall end (the *telos*) of human dignity. These arguments go beyond consideration of the duties we owe to each other to include consideration of the general conditions that are necessary to human flourishing.
30. Arnold Simmel, "Privacy is not an Isolated Freedom" in J Roland Pennock & John W Chapman, eds, *Nomos XIII: Privacy* (New York: Atherton Press, 1971) 71 at 73, as cited in Hunt, *supra* note 3 at 212.
31. Bloustein, *supra* note 7 at 1003.
32. This account of Jourard's work is based on Hunt, *supra* note 3.
33. Sidney M Jourard, "Some Psychological Aspects of Privacy" (1966) 31:2 Law & Contemp Probs 307 at 310–11, emphasis in original, as cited by Hunt, *supra* note 3 at 211.

34. Reiman, *supra* note 12, referencing Erving Goffman, *Asylums* (New York: DoubleDay Anchor, 1961), pp. 1–124.
35. Reiman, *ibid.* at 41, citing Goffman, *ibid* at 29.
36. See, e.g., the analyses of Solove, "Taxonomy", *supra* note 3; Hunt, *supra* note 3; Lindsay, *supra* note 3; and Morehouse, *supra* note 3.
37. *Campbell v MGN Ltd*, [2004] UKHL 22, [2004] 2 AC 457 at para 12 per Lord Nichols.
38. Fried, *Privacy*, *supra* note 10.
39. *Supra* note 11.
40. James Rachels, "Why Privacy is Important" (1975) 4 Phil & Publ Aff 323.
41. Ruth Gavison, "Privacy and the Limits of Law" (1980) 89:3 Yale LJ 421.
42. *Supra* note 30.
43. Fried, *Privacy*, *supra* note 10 at 477.
44. This account of Fried's arguments is derived from the analysis presented by Hunt, *supra* note 3.
45. Rachels actually acknowledges that his arguments about the nexus between privacy and friendship are similar to that of Fried. See Rachels, *supra* note 40 at note 3.
46. *Ibid.* at 331.
47. Article 17(1) of the International Covenant on Civil and Political Rights states that "[n]o one shall be subjected to arbitrary or unlawful interference with his privacy, family, home or correspondence, nor to unlawful attacks on his honour and reputation." *International Covenant on Civil and Political Rights*, 19 December 1966, 999 UNTS 171.
48. *Coeriel and Aurik v The Netherlands*, United Nations Human Rights Committee, 52nd sess, [10.2], UN Doc CCPR/C/52/D/453/1991 (1991).
49. Article 8 states, "Everyone has the right to respect for his private and family life, his home and his correspondence." See Council of Europe, European Convention for the Protection of Human Rights and Fundamental Freedoms, as amended by Protocols Nos. 11 and 14, 4 November 1950, ETS 5.
50. *Von Hannover v Germany*, No 59320/00, [2004] VI ECHR, [2004] 21 EMLR 379 at 50.
51. Zulkiplee Othman, Rosemary Aird, and Laurie Buys, "Privacy, modesty, hospitality, and the design of Muslim homes: A literature review" (2015) 4:1 Frontiers of Architectural Research 12 at 15, citations omitted, available at: https://doi.org/10.1016/j.foar.2014.12.001.
52. *Ibid.*
53. *Ibid.*
54. *Ibid.* See also Besim Hakim, "Mediterranean Urban and Building Codes: Origins, Contents, Impact and Lessons" (2008) 13:1 Urban Des Int 21, https://doi.org/10.1057/udi.2008.4.
55. Nahum Rakover, *Hahagana al Tzin'at haPrat, Protection of Privacy in Jewish Law,* English summary, The Jewish Legal Heritage Society, 2006: http://www.mishpativri.org.il/english/pratiut_english.pdf at xxii-xxiii ("Rakover").
56. Elie Spitz, "Pointers for American Legislation on Computer Privacy: Insights from Jewish Law" (1987) 2 National Jewish L Rev 63 at 70-71.
57. Rakover, *supra* note lv at xxiv.
58. Alan Webber, "Building Regulation in the Land of Israel in the Talmudic Period" (1996) 27:3 Journal for the Study of Judaism in the Persian, Hellenistic, and Roman Period 263 at 275.

59. *Ibid.* at 280.
60. Spitz, *supra* note 56 at 71-72; Rakover, *supra* note 55 at xii; Leviticus 19:16; and Proverbs 11: 13.
61. See the NIV Biblical interpretations of Leviticus 19:16 and Proverbs 11: 13.
62. For clarity, I do not take "autonomous moral decision making" to mean strictly "being rational" or "capable of reason". The human mind and psyche are highly complex, and reason is but one form of exercising the mind, albeit one that is richly valued in some cultural contexts. But the human mind should not be understood strictly in terms of the traditional Western view of reason. "Autonomous moral decision-making" means, for my purposes, having thoughts and preferences, and does include things as simple as liking somethings and not others.
63. See, e.g., Hyman Gross, "Privacy and Autonomy" in J Roland Pennock & John W Chapman, eds, *Nomos XIII: Privacy* (New York: Atherton Press, 1971) 169; Alan F Westin, "Science, Privacy and Freedom: Issues and Proposals for the 1970s" (1966) 66:6 Colum L Rev 1003 ("Science"); Alan F Westin, *Privacy and Freedom* (New York: Antheneum, 1967) ("*Freedom*"); and WL Weinstein, "The Private and the Free: A Conceptual Inquiry" in J Roland Pennock & John W Chapman, eds, *Nomos XIII: Privacy* (New York: Atherton Press, 1971) 27.
64. See Hunt, *supra* note 3 at 212-213 for a good review of scholarship on this point.
65. Solove, "Taxonomy", *supra* note 3 at 551.
66. 1988 CanLII 10 (SCC), [1988] 2 SCR 417 at para. 16 per LaForest J.
67. 19 St. Tr. 1029, 1 Wils. K.B. 275.
68. JS Mill adopted the distinction between the public and private in his philosophical writings, stating that "That there is, or ought to be, some space in human existence thus entrenched "around", and sacred from authoritative intrusion, no one who professes the smallest regard to human dignity will call in question...". The real question according to Mills, is determining how big this realm of private individual authority should be. See Mill, in Mill, J.S., ed., *Principles of Political Economy*, Vol. 2 (London:, University of Toronto, 1965) at 938.
69. Lindsay, *supra* note 3 at 138.
70. *Ibid.*
71. See, e.g., Eric Barendt, "Privacy and Freedom of Speech" in Andrew T Kenyon and Megan Richardson, eds, *New Dimensions in Privacy Law: International and Comparative Perspectives* (Cambridge: Cambridge University Press, 2006) 11 at 23–30; Daniel J. Solove, *The Virtues of Knowing Less: Justifying Privacy Protections Against Disclosure* (2003) 53 DUKE L.J. 967 at 990–92 ("Virtues"); and Solove, "Taxonomy", *supra* note 3 at 513–14. But see Geoffrey Gomery, "Whose Autonomy Matters? Reconciling the Competing Claims of Privacy and Freedom of Expression" (2007) 27:3 LS 404.
72. Solove, "Virtues", *ibid.*
73. See, e.g., Gavison, *supra* note 41; Solove, "Taxonomy" *supra* note 3 at 553-558; Paul M. Schwartz, *Privacy and Democracy in Cyberspace*, (1999) 52 Vand L Rev 1609 at 1656; and Julie E. Cohen, *Examined Lives: Informational Privacy and the Subject as Object*, (2000) 52 Stan L Rev 1373.
74. See Hunt *supra* note 3 at 216–217.
75. "Solitary Confinement", Penal Reform International: https://www.penalreform.org/issues/prison-conditions/key-facts/solitary-confinement/ (accessed Dec. 14, 2019).

76. See, e.g., Stuart Grassian, "Psychiatric Effects of Solitary Confinement" (2006) 22 Wash. U. J.L. & Pol'y 325; Peter Scharff Smith, "The Effects of Solitary Confinement on Prison Inmates: A Brief History and Review of the Literature" (2006) 34 *Crime and Justice* 441; Craig Haney, "The Psychological Effects of Solitary Confinement: A Systematic Critique" (2018) 47 *Crime and Justice* 47 365.

77. Grassian, *ibid.* at 328.

78. See, e.g., United Nations Standard Minimum Rules for the Treatment of Prisoners (the Nelson Mande!a Rules), UNGAOR, 70th Sess, UN DocA/Res/70/175 (17 December 2015); UN General Assembly, *United Nations Rules for the Protection of Juveniles Deprived of Their Liberty : resolution / adopted by the General Assembly*, 2 April 1991, A/RES/45/113; UN Special Rapporteur on Torture report on Solitary Confinement, submitted to the General Assembly, 5 August 2011. UN Doc Number: A 66/268; The Convention against Torture and Other Cruel, Inhuman or Degrading Treatment or Punishment, 10 December 1984, UNTS 1465 (entered into force 26 June 1987); the Istanbul Statement on the Use and Effects of Solitary Confinement adopted by a panel of experts at the International Psychological Trauma Symposium (9 December 2007).

79. Rebecca Green, "Privacy and Domestic Violence in Court", (2010) 16 Wm. & Mary J. Women & L. 237, https://scholarship.law.wm.edu/wmjowl/vol16/iss2/2 at 240–241.

80. *Ibid.* at 241, citations omitted. Green notes that feminist scholars have recognized that historically, women with privilege tended to relegated to the private or domestic realm, while there has always been a class of women who were forced to work outside the home and were therefore at least partially situated in the "public realm".

81. *Ibid.* at 242.

82. *Ibid.*, citing *State v. Rhodes*, 61 N.C. (Phil.) 453 at 457 (1868).

83. *Ibid.* at 252, citations omitted.

84. It turns out that it is not as easy as one would think to determine the "why" parts of our day. Digital technology is good at discerning correlations, but it struggles with causation.

85. For a good overview of big data and its implications for business practices and strategy, see: Ioanna D. Constantiou & Jannis Kallinikos, "New Games, New Rules: Big data and the changing context of strategy" (2015) 30:1 J Info Tech 44.

86. See, e.g., Steve Lohr, "The Age of Big Data" *New York Times* online (February 11, 2012): https://nyti.ms/2jCFuqJ.

87. World Economic Forum, "Big Data, Big Impact: New Possibilities for International Development" (2012): https://www.weforum.org/reports/big-data-big-impact-new-possibilities-international-development/.

88. *Ibid.* at 3.

89. Shoshana Zuboff, "Big other: surveillance capitalism and the prospects of an information civilization" (2015) 30 J Info Tech 75 ("Big Other") and Shoshana Zuboff, *The Age of Surveillance Capitalism: The Fight for a Human Future at the New Frontier of Power* (New York: PublicAffairs, 2019) (*Surveillance Capitalism*).

90. Sarah Myers West, "Data Capitalism: Redefining the Logics of Surveillance and Privacy" (2019) 58:1 Business & Society 41.

91. Karen Yeung, "Five fears about mass predictive personalization in an age of surveillance capitalism" (2018) 8:3 Int'l Data Priv L 258.
92. "Professor Shoshana Zuboff on Surveillance Capitalism: Q&A" (undated), Nesta: findingctl: visions for the future internet: https://findingctrl.nesta.org.uk/shoshana-zuboff/ ("Nesta interview"). See also Zuboff, *Surveillance Capitalism*, supra note 89.
93. Myers West, *supra* note 90 at 31.
94. *Ibid.*; Zuboff, *Surveillance Capitalism*, supra note 89; and Zuboff, Nesta interview, *supra* note 94.
95. Yeung, *supra* note 91 at 259.
96. See Zuboff, *Surveillance Capitalism*, supra note 89 and Zuboff, Nesta interview, *supra* note 94.
97. AI Now Institute, "AI in 2019: A Year in Review: The Growing Pushback against Harmful AI" (October 9, 2019), Medium: https://medium.com/@AINowInstitute/ai-in-2019-a-year-in-review-c1eba5107127. See also AI Now Institute, *2019 Report* (December 2019): https://ainowinstitute.org/AI_Now_2019_Report.pdf.
98. Yuan Yang & Madhumita Murgia, "How China cornered the facial recognition surveillance market" (December 9, 2019) *Los Angles Times* online: https://www.latimes.com/business/story/2019-12-09/china-facial-recognition-surveillance.
99. Kari Paul, "Amazon's doorbell camera Ring is working with police – and controlling what they say" (Aug. 30, 2019), *The Guardian*, online: https://www.theguardian.com/technology/2019/aug/29/ring-amazon-police-partnership-social-media-neighbor.
100. *Ibid.*
101. *Ibid.*
102. Hanna Kozlowska, "Are neighborhood watch apps making us safer?" (October 29, 2019) *Quartz*, online: https://qz.com/1719954/mobile-phone-apps-like-citizen-aim-to-curb-neighborhood-crime/.
103. *Ibid.*
104. Sam Levin, "Racial Profiling via NextDoor.com" (October 7, 2015) *East Bay Express*, online: https://www.eastbayexpress.com/oakland/racial-profiling-via-nextdoorcom/Content?oid=4526919.
105. Westin, *Freedom*, supra note 63 at 35.
106. Sara Bannerman, "Relational privacy and the networked governance of the self" (2019) 22:14 Information, Communication & Society, 2187, https://doi.org/10.1080/1369118X.2018.1478982 at 2188, citations omitted.
107. See Myers West, *supra* note 90 for a good discussion of the ways that the practices of data capitalism are kept hidden.
108. See Aleecia M. McDonald & Lorrie Faith Cranor, "The Cost of Reading Privacy Policies" (2008) 4:3 I/S: A J L & Pol'y for the Information Society 543.
109. See Jonathan A. Obar & Anne Oeldorf-Hirsch, "The biggest lie on the Internet: ignoring the privacy policies and terms of service policies of social networking services" (2018) Information, Communication & Society, DOI:nonbreakingspace10.1080/1369118X.2018.1486870.
110. Aaron Smith, "Half of online Americans don't know what a privacy policy is" (December 4, 2014) Pew Research Center: https://www.pewresearch.org/fact-tank/2014/12/04/half-of-americans-dont-know-what-a-privacy-policy-is/.

111. For a good analysis of the limitations of individuals to engage in effective "privacy self-management" and the complexities surrounding using consent to manage privacy, see Daniel Solove, Introduction: Privacy self-management and the consent dilemma (2013) 126:7 Harv L Rev 1880.

112. Brooke Auxier & Lee Rainie, "Key Takeaways on Americans' views about privacy, surveillance and data-sharing" (Nov. 15, 2019) Pew Research Center: https://www.pewresearch.org/fact-tank/2019/11/15/key-takeaways-on-americans-views-about-privacy-surveillance-and-data-sharing/.

113. Ibid.

114. Ibid.

115. Ibid.

116. Ibid.

117. See the discussion of surveillance capitalism above.

118. See Owen C. King, "Presumptuous aim attribution, conformity, and the ethics of artificial social cognition" (2019) Ethics and Information Technology, https://doi.org/10.1007/s10676-019-09512-3.

119. For a good explanation and analysis of how nudging works and why it is so powerfully manipulative in the context of digital technology, see Yeung, *supra* note 91; Karen Yeung, "'Hypernudge': Big Data as a Mode of Regulation by Design" (2017) 20 Information, Communication and Society 118; Karen Yeung 'Nudge as Fudge' (2012) 75 Modern Law Review 122; and Marjolein Lanzing, "'Strongly Recommended' Revisiting Decisional Privacy to Judge Hypernudging in Self-Tracking Technologies' (2018) Philosophy and Technology 1.

120. King, *supra* note 118.

121. Zuboff, "Big Other" *supra* note 89 at 85.

122. Ibid. at 82.

123. King, *supra* note 118.

124. See Yeung, *supra* note 91 at 259-260.

125. See, e.g., Virginia Eubanks, *Automating Inequality: How High Tech Tools Profile, Police, and Punish the Poor* (New York: St. Martin's Press, 2017); Safiya U. Noble, *Algorithms of Oppression: How Search Engines Reinforce Racism* (New York: NYU Press, 2018); Cathy O'Neil, *Weapons of Math Destruction: How Big Data Increases Inequality and Threatens Democracy* (New York: Broadway Books, 2016);Sara Wachter-Boettcher, *Technically Wrong: Sexist Apps, Biased Algorithms, and Other Threats of Toxic Tech* (New York: W.W. Norton, 2017); and Ruha Benjamin, *Race After Technology* (Meaford: Polity Press, 2019).

126. Amit Datta, Michael Car Tschantz & Anupam Datta, 'Automated Experiments on Ad Privacy Settings' (2015) 1 Proceedings on Privacy Enhancing Technologies 92.

127. Yeung, *supra* note 91 at 264.

128. Karolina La Fors, Bart Custers and Esther Keymolen, (2019) "Reassessing values for emerging big data technologies: integrating design-based and application-based approaches" 21 Ethics and Information Technology (2019) 209 at 219.

CONTRIBUTORS

Yelena Mazour-Matusevich, Ph.D. (1998), University of Illinois at Urbana-Champaign, second doctorate in History, 2018, EHESS, Paris, France. Professor of French and History at the University of Alaska Fairbanks. Published two books, one in French, *The Golden Age of French Mysticism*, (Paris-Milan: 2004) and one in English, *Saluting Aron Ya. Gurevich: Essays on History, Literature and Other Subjects*, (Leiden, Brill: 2010), over 50 essays and academic articles and hundreds of short stories. Second career as an artist. Collaborates with Crosscurrents since 2008.

ymatusevich@alaska.edu

Eric Santanen is Associate Professor of Information Systems in the Freeman College of Management at Bucknell University. He holds both bachelor's and master's degrees in Computer Science from the New Jersey Institute of Technology and a Ph.D. in Management with a major in Management Information Systems from the University of Arizona. In his early career, Eric was a corporate software engineer for a variety of organizations in the financial and pharmaceutical industries. His teaching and research streams have always focused on the ways in which information systems impact individuals, organizations, and society. Over the past several years, this interest has narrowed to focus exclusively on detrimental impacts of technology on individuals and on society, particularly in the area of privacy.

eric.santanen@bucknell.edu

David B. Couturier, OFM. Cap., is Associate Professor of Theology and Franciscan Studies and the Director of the Franciscan Institute at St. Bonaventure University in Western New York

dcouturi@sbu.edu

Taraneh R. Wilkinson received her Ph.D. in Religious Pluralism at Georgetown University, where she also taught. She has recently completed a post-doctoral fellowship at the John XXIII Foundation for Religious Studies (Fscire).

trw28@georgetown.edu

Theresa E. Miedema is Associate Teaching Professor in the Faculty of Business & I.T. at Ontario Tech University. Her research interests include the law and ethics related to technology, privacy, and big data. Dr. Miedema is part of the Anglican community in Toronto, Ontario.

theresa.miedema@ontariotechu.ca

Special thanks go to Katelyn Bushnell, graduate student at University of Bayreuth, Germany, for her help in proofreading the issue.

www.ingramcontent.com/pod-product-compliance
Lightning Source LLC
Chambersburg PA
CBHW040300170426
43193CB00020B/2957